PENGUIN GARDENING

ENGLISH COTTAGE GARDENS

Edward Hyams was well known as an authority on gardening and was one of England's leading viticulturists. He contributed regularly to the *New Statesman*, the *Illustrated London News* and other journals. He was the author of many books, both novels and non-fiction, among them *The English Garden* (with photographs by Edwin Smith), *Dionysus: A Social History of the Wine Vine* and *Great Botanical Gardens of the World*. Edward Hyams died in 1975.

Edwin Smith trained as an architect but shortly afterwards gave up architecture for painting. He took up photography by chance and was encouraged to pursue it seriously by Paul Nash, who was particularly impressed by his work, and by Peter Gregory, founder of the Arts Council. Since then his work has become well known, and there have been many exhibitions of his photographs. He published well over thirty books, the subjects of which include landscape and ecclesiastical and domestic architecture. Among them are *The English House Through Seven Centuries* (written by his wife, Olive Cook) and *Divine Landscapes* (written by Ronald Blythe). Both are published in Penguins. He died in 1971.

English Cottage Gardens

Edward Hyams

with photographs by Edwin Smith

PENGUIN BOOKS

Penguin Books Ltd, Harmondsworth, Middlesex, England
Viking Penguin Inc., 40 West 23rd Street, New York, New York 10010, U.S.A.
Penguin Books Australia Ltd, Ringwood, Victoria, Australia
Penguin Books Canada Ltd, 2801 John Street, Markham, Ontario, Canada L3R 1B4
Penguin Books (N.Z.) Ltd, 182–190 Wairau Road, Auckland 10, New Zealand

First published by Whittet Books 1970
Published in Penguin Books 1987

Made and printed in Hong Kong by
South China Printing Co.

Frontispiece: The marigolds at ALDWORTH, BERKSHIRE, may be descendants of flowers grown when the cottage was built (probably in the late 16th or early 17th century), for by that time they had become some of the commonest garden plants.

Opposite: The tiny front garden of this cottage at GREAT TEW, OXFORDSHIRE, illustrates the cottager's gift for making the most of odd corners and limited space.

For Alan and Jean Jackson, with love

Contents

Colour Plates

Overleaf:
An enchanting
elaboration of old
cottage garden planting
in the style of Gertrude
Jekyll at LITTLE
BARRINGTON,
OXFORDSHIRE.

[1]
Origins

The principal historians of the English garden have virtually nothing to say about the cottage garden before Gertrude Jekyll 'discovered' it during the second half of the nineteenth century as a source of ideas for larger gardens. Their interest has very properly centred on the origins and growth of the art of laying out gardens and the science of horticulture: that being so, they have sought their material in the great gardens, first of the Romano-British villas, then of the monasteries, the castles and the great country houses of the nobility and gentry. And, of course, it was in the great gardens of the rich and mighty, and not in the little gardens of the poor and humble, that both the art of gardening and the science of horticulture developed.

But there is another reason why we find so little about early cottage gardens in the garden histories: there are no, or very very few, documents of any kind. So that if historians have so little to say about cottage gardens until almost modern times, it is for the best of all possible reasons: it is very difficult to find out anything about them. For the whole period of time before the seventeenth century, and one might almost say the eighteenth, we have only hints and fragments; it rarely occurred to garden writers, diarists or economists to notice the poor man's garden. And the great social historians seem to be in no better case, although his small garden must always have been of the very greatest importance, even economically, to the poor man; yet even in so considerable a work as G. M. Trevelyan's four-volume *English Social History*, I doubt whether there are fifty lines about the cottage garden, and there are certainly fewer than that for the cottage garden in the Middle Ages.

Moreover, until the time of John Claudius Loudon, say the mid nineteenth century, the leading professional experts, whether artists like Wise, Kent, Capability Brown and Humphry Repton, or the scientific horticulturists, gave their attention only to the great gardens of the rich. The small gardener received no help from the experts. I know of only one case of a cottage garden designed and laid out by a great garden artist before the nineteenth century: Humphry Repton designed and planted a garden at his own cottage in the village of Hare Street in Essex. We shall see what he made of it, in the right place.

If there were anything in the nature of a cottage garden, or anything which could possibly be so-called, in pre-Roman Britain, we know absolutely nothing about it. In some tribal societies which have survived into our own times, households do cultivate small vegetable gardens in plots of land adjoining or near to their huts; possibly there was something of the kind in some parts of tribal Britain before the Claudian conquest. What I do think probable is that those plants which are commonly supposed to have been introduced after the conquest, for the gardens of the villas which were built for Roman civil and military officers, were in fact introduced earlier. It is probable that the Belgic people of the south-east, who were in religious and trading contact with France, that is to say with a Romanized Gaul, were cultivating such Roman garden plants as cabbage and broad bean, globe artichoke and onion, asparagus and leek, cucumber and grapevine, improved cultivars of apple and pear and perhaps even cherry. The same people may also have had, in the relatively civilized communities of the extreme south-east, such Roman medicinal herbs as valerian, and such culinary herbs as fennel and thyme, before the Roman occupation.

The Roman garden in England, ancestral to the great country-house garden, cannot, either in its shape or its purpose, be thought of as a forerunner of the cottage garden. It was, as described in the letters of the younger Pliny, a gentleman's garden of groves, plantations and vistas, fountains and summer-houses. It had no descendants in England at all: the garden vanished from England with the Romans; when gardens were made again here, they were of quite a different kind, the useful gardens of conventual establishments; and it was not until the English gentry began to make gardens in the Italian manner, that the 'Roman' garden reappeared in England.

The Saxon nobility had gardens, of course; for Bede (c.AD734) says that grapevines were grown in some places; and if the vine had survived the post-Roman chaos, then certainly hardier plants would have done so. We can be a little more specific than that: when a plant unfamiliar to a country is introduced, with it comes its exotic name, which in due course is, like the plant itself, naturalized and becomes a part of the vernacular. Quite a list of plant names having a Latin origin can be traced in Anglo-Saxon: I give the list in English: [1]

Almond; beet; box; hemp; kale; coriander; chervil; chestnut; cornel; yellow rattle; cummin; cherry; feverfew; fig; fennel; gladden (gladiolus) or iris; lettuce; laurel; linseed, lily; lovage; mallow; mulberry; mint; turnip; poppy; peach; parsley; pear; leek; plum; radish; rose; rue; mustard; onion; elm; vine.

There is, of course, no way of telling which of these plants the Saxons gave a Saxon name to when they found them growing here, formerly introduced by the Romans, when they arrived; and which they themselves introduced, with their Latin names, after they were settled here. Moreover, the presence of, for example, elm in this list suggests that it is not a reliable guide to introductions since the elm is unquestionably a native. But either way, the Saxons must have had gardens to grow their vegetables and fruit in. What we do not know is what those gardens were like, or whether only great men had gardens. But I think it should be said that it is only for want of documents that historians always postpone the revival of gardening in England to Christian, monastic times–specifically, the ninth century–and not because they know for a fact that there were no gardens in England between the fifth and ninth centuries. For my part I doubt whether gardens really quite disappeared with the Romans; and I am inclined to think that under the Saxons even the poor man may have had his small garden. But he may well have lost it under the Normans, whose social organization was much less liberal.

For the cottage properly so-called to come into existence, there had to be, of course, cottagers; that is to say, men who were more or less free and who had small houses and plots of land which they could call their own even though they were not freeholders. This means that for our purposes, in a book which is not a social history, it is not really necessary to look back beyond the middle of the fourteenth century, that is to the Black Death in 1349, for the origin of the English cottage garden; or rather, to its several origins, for they are complex.

The Black Death is important because it changed the economic status, and therefore the social status, of the peasants. The Tartar hordes carried it from the East into Russia in 1346; Genoese seamen carried it from the Crimea to Italy in the same year or in 1347, and the plague was ravaging all Italy a year later. When it reached France, in 1348, it appears to have changed its nature from the pneumonic to the bubonic form; it struck England in 1349. The death-rate was appalling; the populations of whole villages were wiped out; one of the worst by-products of the disease was panic—parents deserted their stricken children, doctors and priests deserted their posts wholesale. When the disease began to subside, at least a third of the population had been killed off. How does this affect the subject of the cottage garden? Before the Black Death manor lands were cultivated by servile labour; not long before the disease struck England, however, servile tenants were beginning to commute service payments for payments in money, becoming what were called 'copyholders'. At the same time there came into existence a class of free labourers whose labour could be hired. The lord of the manor used the money he received in rents from copyholders to pay the wages of the labourers who worked his own land. Because of the scarcity of labour after the Black Death, which meant that harvests rotted in the fields for want of harvesters and the next year's crops were not sown for want of hands, prices soared and the manor labourers could not live on their wages. Government efforts to control both wages and prices failed, as they invariably do, political economists being incapable of learning from history. So landlords were forced to let their lands to tenants, providing them with seed and stock for which the tenant returned an equivalent at the end of his tenancy. The beginning of the landlord-tenant farmer-cottager labourer system is to be found in these post-plague 'stock and land' leases. So that it was really after, and as a result of, the Black Death that the cottager appeared in the English landscape and social system; and with him, the cottage garden.

While on the subject of the social and economic changes which put a plot of land at the poor man's disposal, we may as well deal briefly here with a later movement, that of the enclosures. Under some of the Enclosure Acts the man who had formerly had a share in the common field, which was, of course, inalienable, received a plot of his own which was alienable, a freehold. This was bigger than a mere garden, usually about an acre, sometimes more, and it was meant to be farmed, not gardened. It did not always answer, however, and in the *Torrington Diaries*, for instance, there is an enlightening argument between Viscount Torrington, or rather the Hon. John Byng as he then was, and the landscape gardener Humphry Repton, in which Torrington points out

Origins

that the man who received his small-holding under the new Act could sell it at once, thereby depriving himself of a means of feeding his family, for an immediate sum of money.[2] A great deal of small-holders' land did, indeed, quickly return to the big landowners by this means; but, even in the hardest times, the poor countryman still had his cottage garden, though it was usually 'tied' and he lost it if his employer, the farmer, sacked him.

At all events, in the 1350s poor countrymen began to have cottages and gardens which they could call their own. Were these fourteenth-century peasants, then, the pioneers of the cottage garden? Not really: the making and planting of small mixed gardens had been pioneered by others, and the cottager had at least two good examples which he could follow. His garden plants might and to some extent did come from the surrounding countryside, but a great many came from the monastery gardens. And as to the general plan of

A true cottage garden at BRYANT'S PUDDLE, DORSET, which with its apple tree, box borders and mingled vegetables and flowers, perfectly harmonizes with thatch and cob.

the small garden, in so far as it had one at all, that had its origin not in the country, but in the town.

The first gardens to be developed and planted by the owners or tenants of small houses, town cottages as it were, were almost certainly those of the suburbs of the free cities of Italy and Germany in the early Middle Ages. Thus the suburban garden, far from being a descendant of the country cottage garden, is its ancestor; and older, in all probability, by about two centuries. On the face of it a paradox, in fact this is really logical enough: it was in such towns that there first emerged a class of man who was free and who, without being rich, owned his own small house: a craftsman or tradesman protected by his guild from the great barons, and from the petty ones too. Moreover, it was in the towns, rather than in the country, where the countryside provided herbs and even wild vegetables, that men needed to cultivate pot-herbs and salads. It was also in the towns that there existed a market for market-garden produce, so that demand called supply into existence.

London lagged well behind the Italian, Flemish, German and French free cities in the matter of this bourgeois progress towards the freedom of having a garden; yet, as early as the thirteenth century, well before the Black Death, Fitz Steven, biographer of Thomas à Becket, was writing that, in London:

On all sides outside the houses of the citizens who dwell in the suburbs there are adjoining gardens planted with trees both spacious and pleasing to the sight.

Then there is the monastery garden as a 'source' of the cottage garden; this has been discussed in innumerable histories, so that it will be sufficient to deal with it quite briefly. The gardens of the great conventual establishments of the eighth and ninth centuries had two origins: St Augustine, copying the Greek 'academe' did his teaching in a small garden presented to him for that purpose by a rich friend; thus the idea of a garden-school, which began among the Greek philosopher-teachers, was carried on by the Christian church. In the second place, since one of the charities undertaken by most religious orders was that of healing, monasteries and nunneries needed a garden of medicinal herbs. Such physic gardens were soon supplemented by vegetable, salad and fruit gardens in orders which enjoined upon their members the duty of raising their own food, or at least a part of it. Finally, physic gardens tended to develop, willy-nilly, into flower gardens simply because many of the herbaceous and even the woody plants grown

Origins

for medicinal purposes, or for their fragrance as strewing herbs, had pretty flowers – for example, violets, marjoram, pinks, primroses, madonna lilies and roses. In due course these flowers came to be grown for their own sakes, especially since some of them, lilies and roses notably, had a ritual or religious significance of their own. The madonna lily had been Aphrodite's symbolic flower; it became Mary's; yet its remote origin in horticulture was economic; a salve or ointment was made from the bulb.

Much earlier than is commonly realized, certain monastic gardeners were making remarkable progress in scientific horticulture – for example, in forcing flowers and fruit out of season in cloister and courtyard gardens used as conservatories – which had lessons to teach cottagers as well as chatelains. In the ninth century, Abbot Walafried Strabo had twenty-three kinds of flower in his small private garden, the garden in which he wrote his garden-poem, *Hortulus*

Geranium-filled window-boxes add to the luxuriance of this small crowded front garden at BONSALL, DERBYSHIRE.

English Cottage Gardens

addressed to his fellow abbot, Abbot Grimaldus of St Gall, famous for its many courtyard gardens. At the great Carthusian monastery of Clermont each monk had his own 'cottage' garden behind his cell, and this plan was common to all Carthusian establishments. The greatest of the teaching gardeners of the Middle Ages was Albertus Magnus, who had learned much of his horticultural skill from the sophisticated East. When, in mid-winter 1249–on 6 January to be precise–he received the King of the Romans, King William II of Holland, and his suite, at his monastery in Cologne, he was able to amaze the royal party by showing them flowers blooming and ripe fruit on the trees of his cloister garden which he heated artificially. And if no English monastery had such lessons in advanced horticulture to offer, still they did show how a small courtyard garden, comparable in size and shape with a cottage garden, could have something of everything, the essence of the cottage garden. Thus when William Rufus visited Romsey Abbey, much to the terror of the nuns, the abbess was able to show for his admiration not only herbs and vegetables and salads, but roses and other flowering plants.

But if the proto-cottage gardener learned a good deal, at second, third and fourth hand, not only from the city burgesses, with their little town gardens and suburban gardens, and from the monks and nuns, but perhaps also from those ladies who cultivated 'bower' gardens in one of the castle courts, he was none the less a maker himself; and it was for his own pleasure and by his own skill that he added fragrant herbs to the 'worts' of his cottage plot; and then fruit bushes and trees; and then certain flowers, until at last he had created the cottage garden as we now understand it. This was a small and usually rectangular plot partially shaded by one or two apple trees, more rarely by a pear or cherry tree. In it he grew a mixture of fragrant herbs and flowers taken from the wild, with currant and gooseberry bushes among them, and some wild strawberries. This part was grown after nature, and never hoed, the soil being maintained by the decaying of fallen foliage. In another part, where hand weeding, perhaps even some hoeing, might be done, the cottager grew cabbages, broad beans, leeks and onions. The flowers included primrose, cowslip and oxslip, and from these, by selection, came the modern polyanthus. Verbascums, hypericums and mallows were also introduced from the wild or from other gardens. The cottager not only practised a measure of improving selection among the plants

Topiary was one of the arts cultivated by the landowner which found its way into the cottage garden. A characteristic example at LOWER BRAILES, WARWICKSHIRE.

[8]

in his garden, he did so likewise in the wild; for if he noticed a rarity – a double primrose, for example, or a red violet – he would dig it up and bring it home, with the result that mutants which would soon have been lost were saved and propagated and ultimately distributed to other gardens.

Returning Crusaders have usually been credited, it is impossible to say how reliably, with the introduction of some exotics which early appeared in cottage gardens. Among these are the turk's cap lily, *Lilium martagon*, which actually became naturalized on one or two sites in Kent, in Devonshire and in Scotland; *Lychnis chalcedonica;* and the madonna lily, *Lilium candidum* which, curiously enough, is notorious, even now, for being more at home and more flourishing in cottage gardens than in great gardens. The first cottage garden rose, *Rosa gallica*, was also a very early introduction from the Near East.

The very earliest cottage gardens are usually represented as being entirely disorderly, simply a little meadow of plants all growing together in a sort of artificial ecological community. Maybe; I am inclined to doubt it, though. At all events, if, later, as must surely have been the case, some order was introduced, it would have been of much the same kind as the order maintained in monastery herb gardens: small square or oblong beds separated by a grid of very narrow paths based on one or two broader paths. Following the monkish example, too, such aromatics as lavender, thyme, cotton-lavender and southernwood were used as edging plants.

Thus the cottage garden in the century following the Black Death and to the end of the fifteenth century was probably a miniature wild garden or 'flowery mead', and, beside that, a miniature formal, geometric garden of herbs, salads and one or two vegetables; and the whole would be partially shaded by one or two fruit trees. In this 'reconstruction' I am ignoring the larger part of the poor countryman's plot in which he grew beans for flour and, later, a quarter- or half-acre of wheat, oats, barley or rye.

This thicket of hedge - parsley and hogweed at ANSTEY, HERTFORDSHIRE, accords with the state of the thatch and suggests the disorder from which cottage gardens were created.

[2]
The Revival
of
Gardening

If it be true that the monks and nuns of the fourteenth and fifteenth centuries by precept and by example retaught the craft of gardening to both the cottager and the châtelain, it will be as well to inquire where the regular clergy themselves got their skills and their knowledge of plants and their properties. We ourselves live in a literate age: for gardeners of all classes, professional and amateur, there is not only a large, specialized periodical press, but also an enormous number of textbooks covering the whole range from the very simple to the highly scientific; and, of course, there is also much instruction in gardening by radio and television. The cottager of the fourteenth and fifteenth centuries could not read, of course; but his clerical mentors could, and they were also responsible, in an age which was beginning to feel the need of books but had as yet no printing press, for copying and distributing valuable treatises; and there was a small, but very widely read body of garden literature by which the fourteenth-century revival of horticulture was guided.

This literature was not, at first, new; it was what had been salvaged from the classical past. True, the works of Dioscorides and Theophrastus, Columella and other experts on plants and on cultivation were not known again as such until the Renaissance was in full spate and the tide of learning rising all over Europe; but the teaching of those ancient authors was to be found in certain works by men who had copied it, or at least drawn heavily on it; and who stood, in point of time, somewhere between an age when the great original works were current and the fourteenth century.

One of the books which survived was a *Herbarium* which was probably written in the fourth century AD. Its author was one Apuleius, and he had based his book on Dioscorides and on the *Natural History* of the Elder Pliny. Apuleius' *Herbarium*, both in the original Latin and in an Anglo-Saxon translation,[3] was probably the most widely read

The Revival of Gardening

gardening textbook in fourteenth- and fifteenth-century England; and it is significant of its importance and popularity that an Anglo-Saxon version had been called for. That translation was almost certainly made some time before the Norman Conquest; it is very probable that literacy was commoner in the last period of Saxon rule in England than for more than a century after the Conquest: King Alfred the Great translated Latin works into Anglo-Saxon; King Harold Godwinson could read and write both Anglo-Saxon and Latin; William the Conqueror was illiterate.

But Apuleieus, in Latin, in some kind of English, and in French, was not the only horticultural writer still being widely read in the fourteenth and fifteenth centuries, as he obviously had been in the ninth and tenth. There were one or two English writers who helped to spread the ancients' knowledge of plants and gardening among those who could read, knowledge which filtered down to the cottage gardener, probably through the medium of monastic lay-brother gardeners and manor gardeners. Grosseteste, Bishop of Lincoln, born about 1175, was a graduate of the University of Paris; he had studied the properties of plants and he had kept his eyes open to French methods of cultivating them. However, his horticultural writings were not his original work: they were in part straight translation, in part adaptation and editing of a fifth-century work, the *De re rustica* of Palladius, who himself drew heavily on much more ancient authors. Palladius dealt not only with plants, but with such gardening techniques as grafting–his fourteenth book is devoted to that and is a curious mixture of sense and utter nonsense. So that Grosseteste–Palladius[4] is, as it were, the vehicle by which this craft was conveyed to the twelfth century and later gardeners. Alicia Amherst points out the curious fact that so great was Grosseteste's popularity among gardeners, he was still being read and followed well into the fifteenth century, despite the fact that the craft and science of horticulture had by then quite overtaken him; and practical gardeners knew better than to believe, as he did, that you could make apples grow without cores, cherries without stones. In one respect the illiterate cottage gardener, necessarily an empiricist, here had the advantage over his literate fellow gardener who, being able to read, could more easily be misled by rules based on ancient superstitions and too rarely tested by experiment.

Another English horticultural author of this period (b.1157) was the Abbot of Cirencester, Alexander Neckham, who,

The Revival of Gardening

like Grosseteste, was a graduate of Paris. He was a St Albans man, and at one time headmaster of the school run by the Abbey of Dunstable. He returned to the University of Paris, as a professor, in 1180, but he was back in Dunstable six years later, became Abbot of Cirencester (an Augustinian abbey) in 1213, and died four years later. His contribution to gardening literature is to be found in two of his books: a ten-part poem entitled *De laudibus divinae Sapientiae*, of which Part 7 is devoted to Herbs—betony, centaury, plantain, wormwood, etc.—and Part 8 to fruit trees; and a prose work, *De naturis rerum*, in which he describes what a garden should be like. Since, like all his contemporaries, he drew heavily on the classical authors or on their later editors or plagiarists, all of whom were Italians or Greeks, his work is useless in those parts where, for example, he recommends plants which would have been hopelessly tender in the climate of England. But the herbaceous plants which he discusses are almost certainly those which he himself cultivated in his abbey gardens and of which, no doubt, like gardeners throughout the ages, he willingly distributed seeds and cuttings. Here is his principal list:

The garden should be adorned with roses and lilies, turnsole, violets and mandrake; there you should have parsley and cost, and fennel, and southernwood and coriander, sage, savory, hyssop, mint, rue, dittany, smallage, pellitory, lettuce, garden cress, peonies. There should also be planted beds with onions, leeks, garlick, pumpkins, and shalots; cucumber, poppy, daffodil and acanthus ought to be in a good garden. There should also be pottage herbs, such as beets, herb mercury, orach, sorrel and mallows.

Alicia Amherst cites the Latin herbalist, Macer, probably a contemporary of Virgil, whose *Herbal*, in Anglo-Saxon, remained popular into the fourteenth century, presumably in a new translation in English; and an edition of this work was actually printed in about 1530. A MS. of the Anglo-Saxon version, dated as late as 1440,[7] contains some additional plants, known to the translator, John Lelamour.

A number of other translations were circulating during the fifteenth century – Gilbert Kymer's *Dietary*, addressed to Humphrey, Duke of Gloucester, advising on the herbs one should eat for one's health; Nicholas Bollard's edition of Palladius, to which he added a chapter of his own on the planting and grafting of trees; the so-called *Porkington Treatise*, chiefly concerned with arboriculture and pomology.[8] But now comes the first completely original

The considered disorder of this late summer garden at WAIN STREET, HEREFORDSHIRE, with its irregular paving (not intentionally 'crazy') charmingly evokes the character of the true, unsophisticated cottage garden.

English work on horticulture, and it is remarkable for its sound sense and freedom from the accumulated rubbish of centuries of untried theories.

This work was a didactic poem, its author the aptly named Ion Gardener.[9] The poem was written in the first half of the fifteenth century, or possibly late in the fourteenth, and is entitled *The Feate of Gardening*. Alicia Amherst, a very considerable scholar, judged him, from the language he employed, to have been from Kent. There is nothing in the poem which could not be followed with advantage by a modern gardener. The principal headings are on the planting and care of trees; on grafting trees; on the planting and pruning of vines – there were many vineyards in England at that time; on sowing seeds; on planting cabbages and such greens ('wurtys); on the growing of parsley; on other herbs; on growing saffron. I do not propose to give a full list of the plants which Ion Gardener names in his poem; but they include gentian, lychnis, foxglove, daffodil, cowslip and lily among the flowers (all grown as medicinal herbs); fennel, garlic, mint, sage and parsley among the herbs; hazel, pear, apple and hawthorn among the trees, hawthorn being important under two heads, for its flowers, which were boiled and eaten, and as a rootstock for pears; grapevine and honeysuckle among the climbers; strawberry as the only soft fruit; lettuce among the less familiar salads; leek, spinach and cabbage among the vegetables.

So, then, for those who could read there was no serious shortage of horticultural literature, written teaching, in the fourteenth and fifteenth centuries. With the exception of *The Feate of Gardening*, however, it all had the fault of being rather behind the times, but it was a lot better than nothing. And for the cottage gardener, who could not read, there was the example of those who could, the monks in particular, and who based their gardening on these works. It is true, as I have said, that the cottage gardener sought a great many of his garden plants in the wild, in the woods and fields; but to these natives he could, and did, add exotics that were begged or sometimes stolen from monastery and manor gardens.

That the cottager's garden was very important to him, and for the same reason that it has remained so until very recently, is clear from the writings of Langland – *Piers Plowman*. It is obvious that the poor were, willy-nilly, vegetarians; they could not afford butcher's meat, and if they took game were apt to lose a hand or an ear. So, as Langland says,

The Revival of Gardening

Alle the pore peple pescoddes fetten
Benes and baken apples thei brou te in her lappes,
Chibolles and cheruelles and ripe chiries manye.

And then there is the poor woman who,

Two loves of benes and bran
Y baked for my children.

And again, of the poor cottagers,

With grene poret and pesen to poysonn hunger thei thought.

Largely for this reason, that is, the economic importance of the cottager's garden, a distinction other than the obvious one of size must even so early be made between the nature of the cottage garden and the gardens of monastery and manor. In the first place, the crops which were important to the cottager were not the same as those important to the manor gardener: the cottager had to grow beans, to make flour or porridge, turnips and cabbages; you could live on them, though they would not make you fat; just as later, the same class of gardener had to give a great deal of garden space to his potatoes. But the rich man's garden had to produce strong-flavoured herbs and roots to be eaten in meat dishes and with game; hence an emphasis on all the aromatic herbs, the amount of attention given by the garden writers to saffron, and the importance in the garden of onions, leeks and garlic. The gentry were like Chaucer's Sompnour, of whom it will be recalled that:

Wel lovede he garleek oynouns & ek lekes.

The cottager might, of course, grow these too; but he could not afford them much room, he needed the space for crops to fill his belly with.

A thing which the cottager had to learn from the monastery gardener, who had it from Grosseteste or Neckham, who had it from Palladius or Apuleius, who had it from the Greek herbalists or even from Pliny or better still Columella (who had it from his acknowledged master, Mago the Carthaginian), was when to sow the various kinds of seeds in order to get the best results. Those whose precepts had come down untainted from the great Carthaginian agronomist and gardener, or who followed such sensible modern authorities as Mayster Ion Gardener, were not—it is worth emphasizing this—were not taught superstitious nonsense about sowing seeds only by the light of the waxing moon. Yet such ideas were and, amazingly, still are quite common. Where did they come from? From a lore much older than that of scientists like Dioscorides and Theophrastus; they were a part of the Old Religion, persisting in the witch-cult and the horse-cult;

they were handed down by women rather than by men; in short, they were the original 'old wives' tales'. The four-teenth- and fifteenth-century authorites did give dates for the sowing of seeds, but they were based on a combination of academic science and folk-science, that is on experience well tested. And if a certain saint's day was mentioned in this context, as for example that onion, garlic and leek seeds should be sown on St Valentine's Day, this was not because the saint was supposed to help the seeds to germinate; it was simply a convenient and universally understood way of fixing a correct date: tell any amateur gardener to sow seeds 'about' such and such a time, and ten to one he will miss the proper season; give him a fixed day, and he may stick to it.

If one had to guess at the most important kitchen garden, and therefore cottage garden, crop in the centuries we are here concerned with, one might opt for the cabbage, simply on the basis that it seems to have received more attention from the authorities than any other plant, and is, by the way, a principal subject in all early cookery books.[10] A wide variety of names are used, but probably they all meant the same kind of brassica: caboges, cabogis, caul, kole, wurtys, wortes–all one, unless perhaps there may have emerged local varieties, some of them ancestral to the different kinds of cabbage we grow now.

The great proliferation of vegetable, salad and fruit varieties came much later; yet it was already beginning in the thirteenth century; apples are just apples, or rather costards; but by the fourteenth century varieties were being distinguished, and a cottager might prefer to plant a pome-water rather than a Ricardon, a Blaundrelle or a Queening. Almost certainly there were local varieties not known to us now by any name. The same thing is true for pears; in Chaucer's time the Pergenete pear had recently been intro-duced from Flanders or from France,[11] by way of a change from the older Wardon. Again, it is quite possible that there was a greater variety of kinds than we know: apples and pears were eaten and almost certainly cutivated in all Europe, including England, and above all in Wales, in pre-historic times. Segregation, inbreeding, the selection and propagation of good, local chance seedlings cannot fail to produce new varieties of fruit trees; after all, the thing happens even in our own scientific times, and the very popular Granny Smith apple is a case in point. There can, in short, be no doubt that the apple tree in the Somersetshire cottager's garden, even as early as the fifteenth century, was

Village gardeners were inspired by the great gardens to plant exotic trees such as the weeping willows (*Salix babylonica*) in these riverside plots at WEST TANFIELD, YORKSHIRE.

not the same as the apple tree in the Kentish cottage garden; and that not until communications became very much easier were local varieties carried all over the country.

Apples and pears were the commonest, but not the only fruit trees which the cottager of the late Middle Ages had in his garden. Cherries, introduced by the Romans who had introduced them to Italy from the Near East, were early widely grown, and Langland refers to the time of the cherry harvest as 'chery-time'. A cottage might even have a peach tree, but not very often, for the cottager needed to be sure of a crop, and the peaches of that epoch were of poor quality and not very reliable. On the other hand, it is relatively easy to raise a fruitful peach tree from seed. Of the other familiar fruits, plums were very rare even in the great gardens of the churchmen and gentry and virtually unknown in cottage gardens; not even damsons or bullaces were common until much later. Quinces were luxury fruits and not for the cottager, nor were medlars much grown in the poor man's garden. And this was all good sense: for the one fruit which, eaten raw or, more commonly, baked, could be used as a sub-staple was the apple; and it could be, and usually was, stored for the winter.

The improvement of fruit-tree varieties was much facilitated by the spread from the monastery gardens of the craft of grafting. Apple had to be grafted on apple; but the practice of grafting pear on to hawthorn, which lasted well into the nineteenth century when hawthorn was replaced, as a stock, by quince, was a very ancient one; Ion Gardener recommends it and gives instruction how to do it:

> With a saw schalt thou the tre kytte
> And with a knyfe smooth make hytte
> Klene a-tweyne the stok of the tre
> Where-yn that thy graffe schall be
> Make the kytting' of thy graffe
> Be-twyne the newe and the olde staffe. . . .

Where we use wax or a plastic cover, the old gardeners used clay, worked into an ovoid ball to cover the graft; round that they wrapped damp moss and secured it with a flexible hazel switch by way of a tie. I watched a Spanish gardener in a mountain village on Grand Canary using exactly Ion Gardener's method on lemon trees in 1950. Ion Gardener had no illusions about what you could and could not accomplish by grafting. On the other hand, the academic horticulturists, like Grosseteste, propagated a lot of nonsense about this craft, nonsense which lasted into the nineteenth century and which suddenly cropped up again, in a modernized version, with Lysenkoism in the USSR.[12] It was believed that you could alter the look and taste of fruit by grafting on to stocks quite alien–stocks which, in practice, would reject the scion. Robert Salle, a fifteenth-century pomological authority, recommends grafting apple on to elm or alder to ensure red fruits.[13] The odd thing is that such notions lasted so many centuries, for the gardener had only to try it to discover that it was impossible. But before the botanists began to study and understand the kinship groups of plants (mid sixteenth century) perhaps it seemed no more absurd to try to graft apple on elm than pear on hawthorn. On the whole, the cottage gardener, being illiterate, was less exposed to this kind of bookish ignorance of nature, and guided by the light of experience and commonsense did not waste his time trying to work miracles.

The difference between the crops in a gentleman's garden and those in a cottage garden, already briefly discussed, extended to other aspects of the garden. The cottager might keep his garden neat, but, at all events in the fourteenth and fifteenth centuries, vegetables, salads, fruit and flowers were still grown more or less hugger-mugger; that characteristic was retained, in a lesser measure, for centuries and was what gave the cottage garden its particular charm. But by the fifteenth century the manor or monastery garden had, in sharp contrast, become much more orderly. The different kinds of plants were segregated into separate beds. It is very easy to see precisely what these gardens were like, because the earliest botanic gardens were laid out on the pattern of a monastery physic garden: one, Padua, survives unaltered in shape and layout, just as it was made in 1545; two others, the Clusius garden at Leyden University and the Linnaeus garden in Uppsala, Sweden, are exact replicas of the originals. Cottagers never adopted this kind of pattern even when they had room to do it. Nor, of course, did they adopt such new gardening fashions of the time as the arbour, developed out of the earlier Tuscan 'secret gardens', or 'garden room', cut off from the rest by a dense hedge, or by closely planted trees overgrown with ivy. Nor did the cottage garden have such refinements of the times as turf seats and gravel paths or trellis surrounds.

On the other hand, and although it was primarily a kitchen garden, there is no reason to think that the cottage garden had no flowers in it. It certainly had violets and primroses, for they did double duty, being salad herbs. Among the commonest garden flowers of the time, and therefore likely to be in a poor man's garden, were periwinkles and marigolds. Then roses: the flowers were not uncommonly cooked and eaten,[14] but probably not by the cottager. Also commonly grown were the madonna lily, already mentioned, the native iris as well as the fragrant-rooted oris or white iris, an exotic; cranesbill, daffodil, foxglove, centaury and campion; peony and monkshood. Still, it remains true that the cottage gardener's principal concern in the late Middle Ages was edible crops, not with flowers. And if his garden did have in it some flowers which were not just by-products, like those of the culinary herbs, or edible, like those used as salads, then it was as often as not his wife who put them there, in spite of his argument that they were a bit of a nuisance among his beans and cabbages.

Flowers play second fiddle to the cabbages in a wholly unselfconscious cottage garden at POYNTON GREEN, SHROPSHIRE.

[3]
Tudor Changes

The historian of gardening who is dealing with the great gardens of the rich has no serious problems of documentation; since there have been, from prehistoric to modern times, constant changes in style, ornament and material, he can treat the history of this art in much the same way as an art historian, for example, treats the history of painting. But with the cottage garden the case is different: the poor man's small garden did not, of course, respond to changes in garden art styles, changes due to new or changed relations with Continental countries, improvements in trade relations, and such influences; or alterations reflecting changes in the cultural climate in general. The cottage garden could not change under the influence of the great French garden artist Le Nôtre, as could and did the gentleman's garden; or change again with the rise of the landscape gardening school under the influence of Italian landscape painting. Apart altogether from the question of scale, there is the fact that, for century after century, the purpose of the cottage garden remained the same: to help feed the cottager's family; and since the garden's purpose did not change, the cottage garden itself changed only very slowly and in minor ways, until our own times, when the enormous rise in the standard of living of the common people began to be reflected in the cottager's garden.

Still, there were some changes: and roughly speaking we can place them under one of three principal headings. There were changes reflecting the introduction of new garden crops; changes reflecting the cottagers' economic condition; and changes reflecting educational and technological progress.

What is missing from this list? Obviously, those changes in the style of garden art mentioned above: from the fourteenth to the nineteenth centuries they made very little impression on the cottage garden; and such changes as this did bring about were always belated. Perhaps nothing in the

English Cottage Gardens

whole range of social activity so clearly points up the enormous gulf which separated the poor, the cottager, from the classes of comfortable burgesses and the gentry and nobility, as this fact that the cottager's poverty put him outside the cultural pale, so that he took no part in the, as it were, aesthetic life of his country even in the one field where he might have done so, the garden. Of course, it is not absolutely true that the cottage garden remained totally unaffected by changing styles in garden art: a cottager might, from time to time, introduce a piece of topiary into his garden, or use trellis after the manner of its use in the neighbouring great garden. But what possible bearing on the cottage garden could the works of such artists as John Wise, Le Nôtre, Capability Brown, Humphry Repton, Nesfield, or Peto, have?

None: and when, at last, in the nineteenth century a great theorist in the field of horticulture, John Claudius Loudon, turned his attention to the small garden, he did so first in the towns; so that, once again, it was the suburban garden which began to influence the shape and planting of the country cottage garden. And this happened for the same reason that it had happened in the twelfth century: it was in the towns and not the country that there rose up a class of people who could afford only small gardens, but who could also afford to treat them as an amenity and not as a source of food. Not until the twentieth century was the cottager prosperous enough to do that. Naturally, there were exceptions; a village, or a whole region of the country, might be better off than the average and its cottagers able to please their fancy in their gardens: late seventeenth-century Lancashire is a case in point. Indeed, had this not been so we should never have experienced the curious anomaly of what I may perhaps call 'Jekyllism' – that of the cottage garden having an influence on the great gardens of the rich and on the medium-sized gardens of the urban middle class.

If we consider the changes in the style of the gentleman's garden during Tudor times, for instance, it will be clear that none of them had any effect whatever on the cottage garden at that time; and only minor effects on it very much later. The painted trellis-work fences and bowers were not for the poor cottager, nor the 'mounts' – artificial hills climbed by stairs or by spiral paths which can be traced right back to the prehistoric Mesopotamian *ziggurat*; nor the timber and trellis-work garden galleries; nor the 'knot' type of flower bed, more and more elaborate in design, the English version of

ANSTEY, HERTFORDSHIRE The earliest cottage gardeners used the native honeysuckles as garden climbers and they have remained favourites ever since. The cottage gardener was the original domesticator of the species.

the Italian *ricami* and the French *broderie*. After a very long delay, a simplified version of the knot did get into the cottage garden, as when the cottager outlined a path or a flower bed with clipped dwarf box; and one other Tudor innovation did belatedly make an impression on the cottage garden: topiary.

Topiary is a very ancient garden craft. The Romans learnt it from their Syrian gardeners and it is probable that it was first practised by the peoples of the proto-civilizations of Mesopotamia. The craft was revived in Italy, probably by the exponents of the poet Petrarch's school of gardening, in Tuscany; and at last it reached England by way of France, and became all the rage. That it should, although belatedly, have been adopted by some cottagers whereas other new garden fashions were not, is easily understood: many cottage gardens had hedges in any case, there was no question of having to use valuable space for a plant which provided nothing for the table; and man is a maker of patterns: to impose symmetrical or significant shape on things, even on living creatures, is one of his deeper pleasures. So, since the sixteenth century, topiary has been a feature of thousands of cottage gardens; and it was even preserved, for ultimate revival, by the cottager when his betters, under the influence of the picturesque landscape movement, were all over the country busily destroying works of topiary which had taken decades to perfect. I shall have to revert to cottage garden topiary more than once.

But if the adoption of some new garden fashions, in a suitably simplified form, by the cottage gardener was belated because in early Tudor times he could not afford such graces, innovations in plant material were a different matter, and a few of the newly introduced or newly fashionable garden plants quickly made their way from the manor into the cottage garden. A mid sixteenth-century cottage garden was richer in flowers than one of the mid fifteenth century. Auriculas reached England from Flanders, and although the finer and more delicate cultivars were to become collector's pieces for such specialists as the diarist John Evelyn, the first arrivals were the hardy kinds for the knot or border, and ideal cottage plants. Other newcomers included some which we should now think of as typical cottage garden flowers and which did, fairly soon, turn up in cottage gardens: sweet williams, for example, wallflowers, stocks and cornflowers.

There were other Tudor introductions which did not make and never have made their way into cottage gardens:

the common asphodel is an interesting case in point; it was introduced at about this time, but what did it offer the cottager? It has no scent and very little colour; only to the gentleman of education was it endeared by classical associations of which the cottager knew nothing. On the other hand, he found room for the newly introduced white 'poet's narcissus', and the new double daisies from France.

Needless to say, the cottager did not buy his new plants; he got them as best he could, usually, no doubt, from his friend the under-gardener up at the manor house. A few seasons would be enough to spread, from a single root or bulb, a new plant, by divisions or offsets or cuttings, all over a rural neighbourhood. And new varieties of vegetables, salads and fruit spread by the same means, gifts of seed, scion or root.

During the first half of the sixteenth century the cottage gardener lost the man who had for centuries been his best friend, mentor and teacher: the monastery gardener. At the time of the Dissolution there were more than 700 religious houses in England, most of them with gardens. Between 1534 and 1540, in only six years, over 200 were suppressed or surrendered to the Crown. In most cases their gardens, and in all cases their gardeners, vanished. In due course new manor gardens replaced the old monastery ones; but for the time being the cottager had lost a source of plants and horticultural advice which had been invaluable. It was only fortunate that the Dissolution had not happened a century earlier; for now sources of gardening information and material were growing more numerous, and if the cottager could no longer turn to the brother or lay-brother gardener at the monastery, he could turn to the under-gardeners up at the big house, and perhaps, even, if he were not too high and mighty a man, to the head gardener. From the thirteenth to the twentieth century there has been this filtering down of both garden skills and plant material from the big house to the cottage; but from the late eighteenth century it became less important as a popular horticultural press began to cater for a newly literate poor.

The cottage garden continued unaffected by change manifest in such great Tudor creations as Hampton Court, Wanstead, Waltham, Oatlands, Woodstock and many other new gardens. But as more and more new plants reached England, some of them continued to enrich the cottage garden flora. This by no means meant that the old ways of getting garden plants from the wild were given up. Thomas

Philadelphus, Mock
Orange, in a small
LONDON garden. This
flowering shrub was a
Tudor introduction.

Tusser,[15] the most popular horticultural writer of this epoch, advises the housewife:

> *Wife unto they garden and set me a plot*
> *With strawberry rootes of the best to be got,*
> *Such growing abroade among thornes in the wood*
> *Wel chosen and picked prove excellent good.*

So the cottage gardener was still dependent on the little native strawberry. Was the gentleman gardener or the royal gardener any better off? Not for another century were some of the larger American strawberries appearing in gardens; and not until the nineteenth century were the large strawberries we are now accustomed to seen.

But a native fruit which had hitherto been neglected did begin to appear in cottage gardens: the raspberry. It is difficult to see why this excellent fruit had to wait until late in the first quarter of the sixteenth century to be introduced from the wild, but there seems to be no doubt that this was so; and this may be a case where the cottager was the pioneer, the raspberry being established in cottage gardens

Tudor Changes

The ancient art of topiary, revived in pre-Renaissance Italy, reached England in Tudor times. The clipped yew pillars, with their rings and cones give an imposing air to the door at the top of the steps at CODDENHAM, SUFFOLK.

before it was in manor gardens. A plant introduction or domestication, like a geographical discovery or an invention, is not effectively so until it is noticed and recorded, and it is very possible that cottagers had grown raspberries for centuries without the fact being written down and while the squire and the earl were concentrating on exotics from overseas rather than on the natives of their own woods. At all events, the raspberry makes its first appearance in garden literature in 1548 when the herbalist William Turner wrote of it as being found '... plenteously in the wodes in east Freseland ... they also growin in certayne gardines in England'. The same author, by the way, remarks that only in English gardens do you find gooseberries, although they are plentiful in the wild in Germany.

Some of the fruit introductions of this period took a very long time to get into cottage gardens and were, in fact, very rarely planted in them excepting in certain places where an improving landlord took a hand. The apricot, introduced by Wolf, Henry VIII's head gardener, in about 1524, is a case in point. It remained rare in England for half a century, although by 1573 Tusser was including it in his lists of fruits worth planting. But cottagers were quick to seize on new vegetables; the principal staple cottage garden crop had long been the broad bean; now the pea became as important. Tusser advises that they be planted with the beans in January, and he refers especially to the 'runcival' pea, apparently a superior kind.[16]

How were the new varieties of vegetable, and above all fruit, reaching England and making their way from the manor into the cottage garden? Late Tudor England seems to have owed the improvement in orchard and garden tree fruits largely to an enterprising Irishman named, un-Irishly, Richard Harris. He was 'Fruiterer to King Henry eight', and he

...fetched out of Fraunce great store of graftes especially pippins, before which time there were no pippins in England. He fetched also out of the Lowe Countries, cherrie graftes and Peare graftes of divers sorts: Then tooke a peese of ground belonging to the king in the Parrish of Tenham in Kent being about the quantitie of seaven score acres; whereof he made an orchard, planting therein all those foraigne grafts. Which orchard is and hath been from time to time the chiefe mother of all other orchards for those kinds of fruit in Kent and divers other places. And afore that these said grafes were fetched out of Fraunce and the Lowe Countries, although that there was some store of fruite in England, yet there wanted both rare fruite and lasting fine fruite. The Dutch and French finding it to be so scarce especially in those counties neere London, commonly plyed Billingsgate and divers other places, with such kinde of fruit, but now (thankes bee to God) divers gentlemen and others taking delight in grafting . . . have planted many orchards fetching their grafts out of that orchard which Harris planted called the New Garden.[17]

The cottage gardener, like the professional gardener at this time, had a good range of garden tools, much the same as the hand-tools we still use, at his disposal, or at least available to him if he could afford the price, which, as a rule, he could not. Tusser names dibble, rake, mattock (hoe), spade and watering pot. No doubt the lord of the manor found the tools for his gardeners, but the prices of good tools were surely beyond the cottager's pocket. From the Hampton Court accounts in the reign of Henry VIII we know that an iron rake cost 6*d*; a hatchet, 6*d*; a pruning knife, 3*d*; a cutting hook, 12*d*; a grafting saw, 4*d*; and a spade, 8*d*. The highest wage which a rural day labourer, that is to say a cottager, would have been earning at that time was 6*d* a day and it might be as low as 3*d* a day; we will call it 4*d* a day, average; a woman, employed to weed, was paid 2*d* or 3*d* a day. We can make a calculation somewhat on these lines, then; that in Henry VIII's time a garden spade would cost a cottager two days' pay; and taking the farm labourer's wage today (1970) as a basis, this means that the spade cost the man the equivalent of £4 in our money, a pruning knife £2, and a rake £3.

In short, garden tools were extremely dear, far too dear for the cottage gardener unless he might pick one up second hand from time to time. But his usual resource was to make his own tools, or at least those which did not require a smith's skills, equipment and iron. Nothing is more commonly overlooked by people with a yearning for the good old days than the remarkable cheapness of good tools in our own time: a good spade today costs less than half what it cost in 1570; the price of such tools has, in fact, been falling steadily for six centuries.

So, then, the cottager made at least some of his tools with his own hands. Here, quoted from Fitzherbert's *Book of Husbandry*, which was published in 1534, are instructions for making certain garden tools without having recourse to that expensive tradesman, the blacksmith. The work is to be done in winter:

. . . when the housebande sytteth by the fyre, and hath nothynge to do than may he make theym redye, and tothe the rakes with dry wethywode, and bore the holes with his wymble bothe above and under, and drive the tethe upwarde faste and harde, and than wedge them above with drye woode of oke . . . they be most comonly made of hasell and withee . . . . [18]

If he did have to buy some iron tools for working his garden, could not the Tudor cottage gardener recoup himself by making his garden earn him a little extra money by the sale of surplus produce, a practice which was certainly not uncommon in later centuries? There is no evidence either way, but it is not very likely. The kitchen garden crops from his plot were needed to help feed his own family. I suppose that he might occasionally make a penny or two that way, but I cannot really see how it was to be done. Fruit was always readily saleable in towns; but he had no means of getting it to the town market, and in his own neighbourhood everyone was growing his own fruit. Some fruit at this time was very dear indeed: Alicia Amherst quotes, from Tudor

Perhaps this cat and dog
confrontation in privet
at LEVERSTOCK GREEN,
HERTFORDSHIRE, was
suggested by casual
accidents of growth.

household accounts which she consulted, cherries at as much
as 2d a pound and as low as 1d a pound. Now a cottager
might have a cherry tree, although he was much more likely
to have an apple tree or a pear tree. And since you cannot
store cherries, and the cottager's wife did not have the means
to make the preserves which were made by prosperous
farmers' wives or up at the manor, most of the cherry crop
might be sold if there was a local market. I have myself got
as much as £30 (1949 and 1950) for the crop of a small and
virtually wild coppice of Morello cherries. On the other
hand, the prices quoted above–half a day labourer's pay for
one day for a pound of cherries–must have been for prime
fruit of one of Richard Harris's newly introduced Continental varieties. The cottager's cherry tree would not, not yet,
have been that good. And as for his apples or his pears, even
had they not been too valuable to his family as winter store
fruit, they, too, would have been of the older varieties, which,
with market gardeners planting the new pippins and the new
Flemish pears, must rapidly have been becoming unsaleable.

On the whole, cottage garden crops, like the general
character of the cottage garden, remained unchanged in the
second half of the sixteenth century, apart from the fact that
there were a few more flowers and, in some counties, raspberry canes added to the fruits. The principal garden crops were
pulses and cabbages, as before, and the classic aromatic herbs.

We now have to consider a claim, made by some social
historians, that the early Tudor period was a sort of nadir in
the matter of vegetable growing and eating, and that fewer
vegetables were grown and eaten than in the preceding two
centuries, by both rich and poor. This assertion is based on

some positive evidence which has, it seems to me, been accepted rather too uncritically. Here are a few examples: first, William Harrison,[19] writing in the third quarter of the sixteenth century (*c.*1577) says that whereas in the reign of Edward I green vegetables and root vegetables, grown from seed, and some fruits were very plentiful, in the reigns of Henry VII and Henry VIII 'there was little or no use of them in England, but they remained either unknown, or supposed as food more meet for hogs or savage beasts to feed upon, than mankind'. Well, but do people give up a pleasant and wholesome food for no reason? This is one man's remembrance of his childhood; how reliable is it? On what cross-section of society was the assertion based? And does it not read like a generalized exaggeration?

Then there is the opinion of Drummond and Wilbraham[20] that throughout the Middle Ages the poor suffered chronically from scurvy, a condition to be expected if they ate too little fresh vegetables and fruit, since what meat they had was not fresh but salted, and for the rest they had pulses in the form of pudding or bread made of bean flour. But can this be much more than speculative? It might be true locally; it is unlikely to have been true nationally.

Again, there is Robert Child in Hartlib's *Legacie* (1651), who says that some old men remembered 'the first gardiners that came into these parts to plant cabages, collaflours and sowe turneps, carrets and parsnips and to sow Raith pease, all of which at that time were great rarities, we having few or none in England but what came from Holland or Flanders'. Would a villager at the end of the seventeenth century know what was happening all over England? Does this mean any more than that the old men remembered that particular part of Surrey becoming, for the first time, market garden country?

It is perhaps true that there was a decline in the growing and eating of vegetables by the upper classes at the time in question. But it is difficult to reconcile these statements with the other literature, with, for example, Tusser. One should remember that cottage gardeners are very conservative, and would be likely to stick to the garden crops they knew and had tested, even if their betters were, for some reason, giving them up.

What certainly is true is that the influence of Dutch and Flemish horticulture was now very strongly felt; that between 1550 and 1650 it added new vegetables to the English garden flora, as well as new flowers; and that, in due course, belatedly as always, this changed the cottage garden flora, greatly enriching it.

[4]
The
Cottage Garden
Enriched

The new fashions in gardening introduced in the Elizabethan and Jacobean periods, the much increased interest in
gardening as an art among men of wealth, taste and learning –
characterized by, for example, Francis Bacon's *Essay on
Gardens* – again had little or no influence on the cottage
garden. The theorizing of great men on the subject of
garden-making had no bearing whatever on the poor man's
garden plot, which remained what it had been, a kitchen
garden. Even the practical gardening of the rich had no
influence on the shape and purpose of the poor man's
garden; in the long run, of course, improvement in gardening
techniques and enrichment of the garden flora did make an
impression on the cottage garden; but it is important to bear
in mind what, at the time, that garden was. In Elizabeth's
reign the plot of land attached to the poor man's cottage or
hovel was four acres in extent; in short, it was a one-man
miniature farm. Some cottagers might, like the bigger
farmers, embellish their plot with flowers; in fact, they did
so; but primarily at this time, as earlier and later, the
cottager's garden was still a source of food.

English gardening, both ornamental gardening and kitchen
gardening, owed its new liveliness in this epoch, and a
considerable enrichment of its flora to religious intolerance
on the Continent. The persecution of Protestants in France
and the Low Countries drove many skilled craftsmen to
emigrate, and England was their principal refuge; among
these people were skilled, professional gardeners, and they
brought with them not only their superior skill, but seeds
and roots as well. Immigrant market gardeners set up in
business in the neighbourhood of such great cities as London
and Bristol. They grew for sale more kinds of vegetable, and
better varieties of vegetable, than the English of the time –
whatever may have been the case in earlier centuries – were
used to. As a consequence of this new or greatly renewed

The kind of clematis
growing here at
SMARDEN, KENT, was
not seen in our gardens
until after 1840.

market garden trade, beets, carrots, turnips and parsnips were restored to favour on the menu. In due course cottage gardeners began to grow these pot herbs for themselves; slowly and cautiously, for the poor were always reluctant to eat new foods; and because also, at first, seed was scarce and hard to come by. For many centuries the cabbage had been important in the cottage garden; now, at last, the cauliflower, long popular in Flanders and in Holland, joined it there, the first new brassica crop for a very long time. New and better varieties of peas made their appearance in England, and, again in time, replaced the old ones which the cottager had been growing for a century or more.

So that while the enrichment of the flora of great gardens and of market gardens did benefit the cottage garden too, other kinds of garden change did not: the improvement of garden path surfaces, for example, was not at once adopted by the poor gardener; he could not have afforded it; in the big gardens of James I's time there was a greatly increased use of evergreens–*pyracantha*, for example, and even the Italian cypress. This made no impression on the cottage garden, or not for two centuries.

A guide to the enrichment of the ornamental flora of our gardens at this time can be found in Parkinson's *Paradisi in Sole . . . etc.*[21] New introductions of jasmines occurred, there were new exotic clematis for the gardener to plant instead of the native Travellers' Joy. I mention these climbers by way of introducing another climber, of very much greater importance to the cottage garden, and which came into English gardens at this time: the scarlet runner bean. This is first mentioned by John Gerard,[22] who says of the beans:

. . . they do easily and soon spring up and grow into a very great length: being sowen neere unto long poles fastened hard by them or hard by arbours and banquetting places.

From this it is clear that the scarlet runner bean was regarded in England as an ornamental plant; in fact, it seems to have been quite a long time before the esculent quality of the beans was realized. This suggests that the introduction had been so roundabout that the fact of the scarlet runner being a food plant had been overlooked. All these 'haricot' beans–runners, 'French' beans, kidney beans, Lima beans and so forth–of the genus *Phaeseolus* are native of either Central or South America and were unknown in the Old World before the sixteenth century. Important farm and garden crops in both the Inca and Aztec societies,[23] they were introduced into Europe–presumably in the first place

The Cottage Garden Enriched

'Oriental' hyacinths like those in this garden at GAINSFORD END, ESSEX, did not become cottage flowers until long after their introduction in the early nineteenth century. They were among the eight classes of 'Florists' Flowers'.

to Spain by way of the Canary Islands – not as wild plants, but as cultivars of great antiquity. Although, as I have said, they were first grown here as ornamentals, the rich were soon eating the beans; and in due course the cottager started to grow them in his own garden: they are, of course, ideal cottage garden plants, for, while they are indeed ornamental, they also provide a relatively enormous crop of good fresh food. Even so, it is doubtful whether you would have found scarlet runners in cottage gardens before the middle of the next century.

Three major features of Elizabethan/Jacobean gardens, I mean the gardens of great houses, were mazes 'set with lavender or cotton spike, marjoram and suchlike, or Isope and Time or quickset privet, or plashed fruit trees';[24] arbours; and topiary, all of them introduced from the Continent. The only one of these which ultimately appeared in the cottage garden was, as I have said earlier, topiary; happily ignorant of Francis Bacon's pronouncement against it – 'I for my part, do not like images cut in juniper or other garden stuff – they be for children' – the cottager did adopt this garden fashion. How did cottagers learn the skilled craft of clipping and pruning bushes into shapes? Almost certainly by the example and teaching of professional gardening neighbours, men who worked in some great garden, but who were themselves cottagers. These professionals became extraordinarily skilful in this work: as early as 1618 Lawson was writing:[25]

English Cottage Gardens

Your gardiner can frame your lesser wood to the shape of men armed in the field, ready to give battell; or swift running greyhounds to chase the Deere, or hunt the Hare. This kind of hunting shall not waste your corne, nor much of your coyne.

Then, as now, the professional gardener working in a great garden, used his skill and his special opportunities to get good new plants, to embellish or enrich his own small garden. There can be no doubt that, throughout the history of gardening, these professional gardeners' gardens have been an important channel through which newly introduced or newly bred garden plants were distributed from the great into the lesser gardens of England. And garden skills were spread by the same means, including the craft of topiary.

In England we are inclined to think of only two evergreens in connexion with topiary – yew and box. Box is, indeed, the most ancient subject for the topiarist; but yew is relatively new, for the Italians used and still use *Cupressus sempervirens*. There are, of course, many other suitable plants: I have seen *Arbor vitae* used most effectively in some American gardens, for example for the 'wings' of the great open-air theatre at Longwood, Pennsylvania. But at the time we are here concerned with the winter beauty of evergreens seems hardly to have been grasped; and the shrub most widely used for topiary was, of all things, privet. Parkinson says of it in his *Paradisi:*

Examples seen in the nearby garden of the great seventeenth-century house at EAST RAYNHAM, NORFOLK, may have inspired the simple traditional forms of this cottage garden topiary.

The Cottage
Garden Enriched

Because the use of this plant is so much and so frequent throughout all this land, although for no other purpose than to make hedges and arbours in gardens etc., whereupon it is so apt, that no other can be like unto it to be cut, lead and drawne into what forme one will, either of beasts, birds, or men armed or otherwise, I could not forget it. . . .

But Barnaby Googe says that lady topiarists liked rather to cut 'a cart, a peacock, or such things as they fancy' in rosemary.[26] Still, it was certainly privet which the cottage garden topiarist favoured for a long time; and his subjects were drawn not from his own world, but from that of his social betters: his garden topiary was of peacocks, not of crows.

There were two major differences in the ornamental aspect, as between the gentleman's garden and the cottager's garden, and in so far as the latter was ornamental at all, and setting aside the absence from it of such arbours, mounts, mazes, galleries, summer-houses and elaborate trellis-work. The cottager continued (there were probably some exceptions), to plant vegetables and flowers all mixed up – poppies among his cabbages – and only grew the staples really clean. The gentleman's garden was becoming yearly more orderly and formal. The second increasingly wide difference was in the ornamental flora.

As to the matter of the laying out and ordering of gardens, a new fashion made it easier for the cottager to imitate the great garden; yet he certainly did not at once do so. This was the fashion for knots edged not with live plants, but with lead or pebbles or even sea-shells. Lead, of course, the cottager could not afford; but he could collect pebbles. Of their use Parkinson says, '. . . it is the newest fashion and maketh a pretty handsome show'. Very likely some cottagers did begin to order and edge their garden beds in the same way at this time; very much later, almost a couple of centuries, the fashion endured only in cottage gardens. But even so, the order of a cottage garden was not of the kind implied in another aspect of Parkinson's description of a knot garden: he says that the knots demarcated by white or blue pebbles were to be filled with flowers 'All planted in some proportion as neere one unto another as is fit for them'. By this means the garden, he says, 'will seem like a piece of tapestry of many glorious colours'. But that kind of thing was not for the cottager.

Then as to the flora of the two kinds of garden: although by this time there were certainly a few exotics in the cottage garden, on the whole the cottager still relied on native

English Cottage Gardens

English flowers for the bit of colour among the cabbages and beans; to those noted as common in earlier gardens were added a few more: narcissus, fritillary, tulip and hyacinth, of which Parkinson specifically says that they are '. . . almost in all places, with all persons . . .', but adds that they are more commonly seen in gentlemen's gardens. But in the gentleman's garden the exotic flora was growing yearly richer: among the introductions of this epoch, introductions which were not to reach even the best cottage gardens for about a hundred years, were lilac and philadelphus and laburnum; *Lobelia cardinalia* from North America, and Crown Imperial from the Near East; exotic hellebore, cyclamen, sunflower and some new campanulas. Very slowly, by the usual route, these began to make their way down the social ladder.

It was about this time that the so-called Jerusalem artichoke first appeared in the kitchen gardens of the rich and in market gardens. 'Jerusalem', by the way, is a corruption of *girasol*, the plant being a sunflower; and 'artichoke' comes from the fancied resemblance to the flavour of the globe artichoke which had long been in our gardens. As a novelty, the artichoke was highly prized and expensive; but it had rather a short career; the cottager never took to it, although in due course it was urged on him because it produces a lot of cheap, filling foodstuff; and in any case it was, in due course, to be displaced in favour by the potato. Some writers on garden plants dismissed it, almost from the first, as a food fitter for pigs than people. Parkinson, by the way, calls this vegetable 'Potato of Canada', thus,

The Potatos of Canada are by reason of their great increasing, grown to be so common here with at London, that even the most vulgar begin to despise them, whereas when they were first received among us they were dainties for a Queen, but the too frequent use, especially being so plentiful and cheap hath rather bred a loathing than a liking for them.

Parkinson used the word 'potato' in this context because the first tuberous vegetable eaten in England was the sweet potato. So a tuber was a potato, even if it was an artichoke. The ordinary potato was by now being grown by Gerard in his Holborn garden; Gerard calls it 'a meate for pleasure', and suggests that it should be either roasted or boiled, and served with oil, vinegar and pepper. But because the potato was, in due course, after battling for two centuries to overcome the conservatism and prejudices of the poor, to become king of the English cottage garden; and because it was, after the cereals, by far the most important plant introduction

TRESCO, SCILLY ISLES In south-west England cottage garden flora became exotic for climatic reasons.

The Cottage
Garden Enriched

ever made into Britain, I am giving it a chapter to itself, and it need not be discussed any further at this point.

Other vegetables had become increasingly popular and were being widely grown. Holinshead,[27] in whose *Chronicle* William Harrison's *Description* quoted above appears, says that among the 'poor commons' the use had been resumed of '. . . melons, pompions, gourds, cucumbers, redishes, skirets, parsneps, carrets, cabbages, navewes, turnips and all kinds of salad herbs'. I do not know what difference there may have been between navewes and turnips; perhaps the navewe (French, *navet*) was the white turnip, and the turnip what we now call the swede. Not all of these, certainly, were grown in cottage gardens. Even the professional market gardeners commonly failed with melons in England until the great days of 'high gardening' and the hot-house. But most of the roots and greens were grown in cottage gardens. The gentry, as Holinshead says, '. . . make their provision yearlie for new seeds out of strange countries'. Thus, they were constantly introducing improved strains from Holland, Flanders and France; whereas the cottagers saved their own seeds; and Parkinson goes so far as to say that when it comes to '. . . redish, lettice, carrots, parsneps, turneps, cabbages and leeks . . . our English seede . . . is better than any that cometh from beyond the seas'.

It is unfortunately not possible to discover how the cottage garden was affected, if at all, in fruit-growing by the large number of new varieties of apple and pear trees which became available towards the end of the seventeenth century. What seems to have happened is that not only were many new kinds introduced from the Continent – rainbures, capandas, calual (calville) and many more – but varieties which had formerly had a merely local repute and distribution – Kentish codling, Worcester apple and other 'county' kinds – became generally available from nursery gardeners whose malpractices, such as selling dead fruit trees, were now, as they became increasingly important with the growth of a nursery trade, checked by the chartering of a Livery Company of Gardeners with strict rules and by an Act of Parliament setting heavy fines.

WENDENS AMBO, ESSEX
First grown in the gardens of the rich, the dahlia's remarkable process of reproduction by root-tubers soon led to its wide planting in cottage gardens.

Not only apples, but other fruits became available in much greater variety. By the end of the century over sixty kinds of pear were in cultivation in English gardens. The ancient Wardon still lingered on in cottage gardens, but some of the newer ones were also planted. It is probable that this figure of sixty is an underestimate; they were probably the good

[43]

kinds; for Gerard says that if the worse kinds were included, '. . . to describe each pear apart were to send an owle to Athens, or to number those things which are without number'. The same author makes a short-list of eight top varieties; if any of them are still in cultivation today, it must be under different names. But the, as it were, semi-generic term 'bon cretien' was in use then as now; and Parkinson mentioned a bon cretien pear called the ten-pound pear – it was the Syon bon cretien – not because the fruits weighed ten pounds each, but because '. . . the grafts cost so much the fetching by messenger's expenses, when he brought nothing else'. Someone had been sent to Flanders for them.

The variety of cherries had increased to over thirty kinds, the counties where they were at their best and most diverse being Kent and Norfolk. By this time the primitive cherries of the Middle Ages had probably disappeared even from the cottage garden; for with the spread of the craft of grafting, it became easy enough to make over an old tree, using it as rootstock, to new varieties, an art I have practised myself. Over sixty kinds of plum and damson were now in gardens, largely as a result of John Tradescant's particular interest in introducing plums. Some few of these had made their way in the cottagers' garden. Gerard names a Mr Vincent Pointer of Twickenham as the great amateur and collector of plums. Apricots became commoner in the gentleman's garden, but not among cottagers; nor were the peaches and nectarines listed by Parkinson as cottage fruits, or the revival of vineyard planting, at this time, in southern England, of interest to the cottager.

Although the poor cottagers of England were the last people in our society to be affected by the slow, but increasingly less slow, spread of literacy – even at the end of the eighteenth century kindly and liberal men like Viscount Torrington (of *Diary* fame) and Humphry Repton, the landscape gardener, were saying that there was no point in teaching the common people of the countryside to read and write – the fact that more and more people could read did mean that there were more and more people able to pass on horticultural knowledge culled from books. Turner and Tusser have both been mentioned and quoted from: Tusser's *Five Hundred Pointes of Good Husbandry*, written during his semi-retirement as a Suffolk farmer, was published in 1557. Herbals became much more common, chiefly translated from the Dutch, French or Italian translations of the Greek and Latin classics – even Gerard's famous *Herbal* was in part a translation from the Dutch of Dodoens.

The paths of 'Picturesque' gardens bend and are called *natural*, but for the cottager the shortest way to the door was the natural one. This straight brick path at TENTERDEN, KENT, is as expressive of the locality as the tile-hanging.

English Cottage Gardens

Here at MELLS, SOMERSET, the cottager makes full use of the space between his house and the country road for plants such as croton unknown to his forebears.

Mathias de l'Obel, who incidentally was called in to correct Gerard's bad botanical Latin, supervisor of the garden in Hackney owned by the great amateur of plants and gardens, Lord Zouche, and later Botanist Royal, published his *Stirpium Adversaria* in 1570: in this he sketched a scientific system of plant classification of the kind already pioneered by the Italian Matthioli at Padua; but as this was in Latin it was available only to the learned.

The amateur but erudite plant collector, who has ever since been an important figure in English gardening, now made his first appearance. A Northcountryman, Thomas Hesketh, collected in Lancashire and Yorkshire, sending plants to Gerard for him to try in his London garden; one Thomas Edwards was doing the same in the West Country. A London merchant, Nicholas Lete, made plant collecting expeditions in both England and France: moreover, so enthusiastic a plantsman was he that '. . . he doth carefully send into Syria having a servant there at Aleppo and in many other countries, for which myself and likewise the whole land are much bound to him' (Gerard). Perhaps, from the cottage gardener's point of view, Lete's most important introduction was the Savoy cabbage, which has remained a favourite in the poor man's garden ever since.

Nor were amateur collectors the only ones at work: Gerard employed a collector in the Mediterranean basin: by that time the Mexican *Opuntia* which we call prickly pear and the French figue de Barbarie had become established there, and Gerard's man sent it to England where, happily, it proved too tender to survive the winter.[28] Other collector botanists were the apothecary Thomas Johnson, MD, whose shop in London was the first to diplay a stalk of bananas in

The Cottage Garden Enriched

the window; he wrote of this fruit, 'Some have judged it the forbidden fruit; other-some the grapes brought to Moses out of the Holy Land.' Then there were John Goodyer, Thomas Glynn; and Ralph Tuggy, who was famous for another flower which became a permanent inhabitant of the cottage garden, the pink, and who also had a fine collection of carnations and auriculas.

Above all there were the Tradescants, grandfather, father and son, to whom the cottage garden, and all other kinds of garden for that matter, owe so much. The eldest of the three was a Dutch immigrant into England in the first decade of the seventeenth century; his son, John Tradescant, gardener to Lord Salisbury, and John's son, the youngest Tradescant, travelled to collect plants all over Europe, into North Africa, and in Virginia. They had their own garden in Lambeth, where they acclimatized their introductions. The younger Tradescant was cheated out of the remarkable collection of natural curiosities built up by the three generations, the so-called Tradescants' Ark, by a rascally attorney named Elias Ashmole, who subsequently presented what was not his to give to Oxford University. The Tradescants not only collected abroad, but they bought seeds and roots in foreign markets for their English patrons. Among the cottage garden flowers they introduced were double daffodils, exotic anemones, and the spiderwort *Tradescantias*. On the other hand, many of their introductions were never of use to cottage gardeners – tulip trees, for example, and the swamp cypress. Incidentally, some of their new cultivars came from the nursery garden of Jean Robin, the greatest practical horticultural botanist of France, whose nursery played an important part in stocking the Jardin du Roi, later known as the Jardin des Plantes.

Some of the most considerable amateur gardeners of the epoch, such as Sir Hugh Platt, but above all Sir Thomas Hanmer, did more than introduce new plants for the cause of the amateur gardener: by experiment and practice they built up a body of skill and knowledge about the cultivation of the new plants; skill and knowledge which, by the process of social osmosis already described, became a part of the corpus of cottage gardening lore.

But with some of the gardener-botanists mentioned or quoted here I have drifted forward into a new epoch of horticulture. Before coming to that, it is time to devote a chapter to the plant which became the king plant of the cottage garden, *Solanum tuberosum*, the common potato.

[5]
Potatoes
and
the Cottager

The potato, *Solanum tuberosum* and other species, is a native of Chile and Peru. Its destribution in the wild is wide, but there is some evidence, not altogether convincing, that the centres from which came most of the potatoes grown in Europe, were the region of Lima, and the island of Chiloe.[29]

Although we call the potato plant *Solanum tuberosum*, it is very likely that the potatoes introduced into Europe in the sixteenth century, being cultivars, contained the genes of related species. For, by the time the Spaniards and other Europeans came across it, it was already ancient in cultivation: domesticated by the pre-Inca nations of the Chilean and Peruvian littoral, and the western watershed of the Andes, it was one of the staple foods of many parts of the Inca Empire up to altitudes as high as 1,200 feet; different kinds of potato were grown in different parts of the Empire, and all of them differed considerably from the parental wild species. Like two other members of the same family of plants, the *Solanaceae* (many of whose Old World genera are poisonous –deadly nightshade, for example, and the thorn apple, *Hyocyanus niger*), tobacco and the tomato, potatoes wrought an economic revolution in the Old World.

So, the potato as introduced into Europe was not a wild plant, but a garden plant; and it must have come from a latitude well to the south of its principal home as a wildling.[30]

It is probable that the first European mention of the potato was in a letter from the Conquistador of Chile, Valdivia, to the Emperor Charles V, in 1551. He mentions it as one of the native crops; but apparently no Spaniard would eat it even when the soldiers were nearly starving; and the prejudice behind this was to crop up time and again before the potato completed its conquest of Europe.

It has not been possible to fix an exact date or place for the first cultivation of potatoes in Europe. Salaman and other authorities seem always to assume that it must have been Spain; but I do not see why: there were men of all Europe

among the conquistadores. At all events, the first mention
of the potato in print was in Gerard's *Herbal* of 1596 and he
must, before then, have been growing it for some time, for he
was clearly familiar with its behaviour. Dr Salaman con-
siders that the fact that Turner, on the other hand, never
even mentions the potato, gives us a datum line 'before which
we may be reasonably certain that the potato was unknown in
Europe'. The last edition of Turner's *Herbal* was in 1562:
this would seem to fix a first introduction between 1562 and
not later than, say, 1590. We can get a decade nearer than
that: for in 1577 was published the last of several editions
of John Frampton's English translation of a work by Nicholas
Monardes, which lists and describes the plant introduction
from the Americans into Europe up to that date.[31] Frampton probably used the 1571 edition of the original for his
work; and that does not mention the potato.

Gerard says that he got his potato tubers from 'Virginia'.
Too much heavy weather has been made by scholars about
how and why he made that mistake; granted that there were no
potatoes in Virginia at that time, I wonder if, to Gerard the
word 'Virginia' meant anything more specific than 'America'?

Almost contemporary with Gerard's account of the potato
in English, is Gaspard Bauhin's in French; and it was
Bauhin who first named the potato *Solanum tuberosum*.[32]
Four years later the great French agronomist and horticulturist Olivier de Serre devoted an entire chapter of his
Théâtre d'Agriculture[33] to the cultivation of the new
vegetable. The French probably had their first potatoes
from Italy; for from Clusius's account of it we know that
they were being grown in Italian gardens as early as 1588.
Salaman assumes that the Italians must have had potatoes
from Spain. I do not follow this: there were many Italians,
especially Genoese, in the Spanish ships; after all, even
Columbus was a Genoese. As to Spain itself, potatoes were
being grown there as early as 1573, which puts the actual
introduction not later than say 1570.[34]

Still earlier dates have been given, but they are not
verifiable; and in some cases they can be shown to have been
impossible. For example, John Hawkins cannot, as according
to one account he did,[35] have introduced the potato into
Ireland in 1545, since at that time he was still a schoolboy·
Probably, in any case, there were several separate introductions; and certainly there were at least two, as witness the
differences between the plants described by, respectively,
Gerard and Clusius. Vavilov specifically calls the plant,

English
Cottage Gardens

which he believed came from Chiloë, 'the Irish potato'; and the fact that Francis Drake was using potatoes as part of his ship's stores at least as early as 1577–the natives of Mocha off the Chilean coast gave him some as a present–is also significant. I shall add another speculation of the kind which professional historians, tied to the documents, dislike: I have said elsewhere that a discovery, introduction or invention is not effective until recognized as such; I can imagine one of the more intelligent conquistadores slipping a potato into his pocket with, in mind, some enthusiastic gardening friend back in the old country; this could have happened at any time after the discovery of Peru; in short, there may have been half a dozen unrecorded introductions of the potato for all we know, and probably there were.

Potatoes and the Cottager

The theory that Sir Walter Raleigh was in some way responsible for the introduction of the potato to Ireland having been reduced to the status of a mere legend by some historians, was restored to respectability by Salaman,[36] who has also shown the part played by Drake in this important economic revolution.

Ireland was the part of the British Isles where the potato first established itself—to the ultimate ruin of the country. It arrived there after 1580 and before 1600. At that time the principal cultivators of the soil in Ireland were the class of 'churls', and they either cultivated their own open-fields ('rundale') in common, or worked, as labourers, on the farms of their clan chieftains. Technically, Irish agriculture and horticulture lagged far behind the English practice. This

The garden at WARBSTOW, CORNWALL (*left*) and the allotments at SAFFRON WALDEN, ESSEX (*below*) are both examples of the cottager's plot in its purest form as the vestige of the Elizabethan five-acre small-holding for the raising of food.

very fact, together with the facts of social and political life in seventeenth-century Ireland, led to the acceptance of the new crop plant, which was so easy to cultivate, which yielded so large a crop for so little labour, and which flourished so well in the Irish climate. Elsewhere in Europe the story was very different, especially in England, as we shall see. The fact is that in Ireland the potato came as a salvation of the common people from a part of their appalling miseries, miseries imposed by an anachronistic social system and a more or less constant state of war with the English and Anglo-Irish.[37] It is notorious that this war was fought with savage cruelty and ferocity on both sides. A food plant which would yield adequate sustenance as quickly and for as little work as the potato was a godsend to a peasantry which was hardly given time, during a hundred years, to lay down the weapons which it had snatched up in self-defence.

In the potato, the weary and harassed cultivator had to his hand a food which was easier to prepare than any of which he had experience; one which would feed him, his children and his livestock out of the same cauldron, cooked on his open hearth of burning turves. There was, I believe, a still greater advantage which it offered; the potato could both be cultivated and stored in a manner which might outwit the spirit of destruction and malevolence of his enemy. Within a few years the Irish cultivators did develop such methods. . . .[38]

As early as 1610 the potato had become a food staple in certain parts of southern Ireland; in the north its adoption was slower, but by the end of the seventeenth century it was the staple food all over Ireland. Here is a brief but vivid description of an Irish cottage garden late in that century:

. . . a piece of ground sometimes of half an acre, and in this their turf stack, their corn . . . the rest of the ground is full of those dearly beloved potatoes and a few cabbages. . . .[39]

So the Irish cottage garden, backward, bleak and flower-less, or nearly so, was the first to be taken over by the potato, whose progress in England was very much slower.

The beginnings of the potato story in England are confused because, long before the common potato became established here, the sweet potato, imported from Spain or Portugal where the climate permitted of its cultivation, and with a great reputation as an aphrodisiac,[40] some of which rubbed off on to the common potato, was eaten by the rich in England as a luxury food; it was often candied. Thus, there are several references to the potato in Shakespeare's plays, but there is no reason to suppose that he had ever

Trellis and an arbour are not commonly found in cottage gardens, but here at SAFFRON WALDEN, ESSEX, they enhance the stylized cottage planting.

Potatoes and the Cottager

seen, or even heard of, *Solanum tuberosum*. There is, in Burton's *Anatomy of Melancholy* (1621), a reference to the potato which could be the ordinary potato and not the sweet potato; if so, it is the first in our non-technical literature.

The common potato was being grown in a few market gardens and in small quantity early in the seventeenth century, for potatoes were being sold in London at 1s a pound (say about 15s to £1 in our money). (Sweet potatoes were three times that price, a ruinous extravagance.) But, a mark of the slow increase in market garden cultivation, by the end of the century the price was down to 1d a pound.

Having, then, made its first English appearance in Gerard's Holborn garden in 1590, the potato was for long confined to a few market gardens catering for the rich, and to the gardens of a few rich amateurs of rare plants: Salaman thinks that Gerard may have planted potatoes in Lord Burleigh's garden in the Strand, which he supervised; and it was quite early in the Tradescants' Lambeth garden. It is included by Parkinson in his lists of kitchen garden plants. But it remained a rarity; so much so that 'it was still a luxury in the kitchen of Oliver Cromwell's wife, Joan'.[41] It seems very remarkable, but it is nevertheless true, that at a time when the potato was swiftly colonizing the Irish cottage garden, it remained unknown to the English cottager. And this despite the fact that, as the fall in price indicates, it was a fairly common market garden crop by mid century; and that it had, by its large yield for little labour, attracted the attention of economists as a possible food for the poor. John Evelyn, although he thought that potatoes tasted like 'an old bean or roasted chest-nut', nevertheless suggested that it could be of 'excellent use for the relief of the poor, yea and of one's own household when there are many servants, in a dear year'.[42]

By 1680 the potato had become more or less familiar to most people in England. In that year, Robert Morison, Professor of Botany at Oxford, one of the century's great scientists and a practical gardener of such talent that even the famous Leyden University Botanic Garden was replanted after the system he had adopted at the Oxford Botanic Garden, wrote that it was a familiar plant in 'most gardens'. But what did he mean? Probably no more than that by then the urban and rural middle class–professional men, substantial tradesmen, prosperous farmers–were growing a few potatoes in their gardens. There is no evidence that they had yet made their way into the cottage garden, although here and there must surely have been cottagers who

The gardens of a whole row of cottages like these at WANTAGE, BERKSHIRE, enliven the scene with their diversity and are at the same time eloquent of a warm spirit of community.

were trying them and urging their neighbours to do likewise: many a small tuber must have been slipped to a villager by a friend who was a gardener up at the great house, in the village inn of an evening. But the rural poor, being, until our own times, the least educated and therefore the most superstitious and prejudiced class in the community, were always the most conservative in the matter of food; very special conditions, like those obtaining in Ireland, were required to break down their resistance to a new food. Salaman quotes the case of starving Neapolitans refusing to eat potatoes, which they were unfamiliar with, and which had been sent as famine relief, in 1770; and in our own time Far Eastern peasants are said to have refused to eat wheat instead of rice even when they were dying of starvation.

But if the poor cottager was still reluctant to plant potatoes in his own garden, there was a sort of conspiracy to force them on him. In 1662 the Royal Society, having discussed a proposition from a Mr Buckland 'to plant potatoes through all ye parts of England' as a protection against famine, the committee considering this concluded:

. . . 1. *that all those members of ye Society, as have land, should be desired to begin ye planting of this root and to persuade their friends to doe ye same. 2. that in order thereunto Mr Buckland should be desired to send up what quantity he could of ye smaller potato's to furnish those, yt have conviency to plant them in order to which Mr Boyle offered to provide as many of them, as he could, as also to communicate such notes of his concerning this root and their diffusiveness as he could recover. 3. yt Mr Evelyn should be desired to insert this proposition and ye approbation thereof, together with ye management and spreading of ym, into ye Treatise which he is now publishing by order of the Society concerning ye planting of Trees. 5. yt provision being made of these roots, ye way and usefulness of planting and spreading ym, should be published and recommended to ye Nation, in ye Diurnalls, without further naming the Society in it, and yt therein direction should be given to certain places, where they may be had for those, yt have a mind to plant ym.*

Boyle and Evelyn were, of course, *the* Boyle and *the* Evelyn. The Royal Society committee took on the responsibility for investigating the proper cultivation and uses of the potato. They were not alone: others were on the same tack, and one John Forster suggested making potato planting a royal monopoly. The potatoes raised by licencees were to be made into bread for the poor, thus releasing more corn for export.[43] Meanwhile, cottagers in southern England were still resolutely keeping the potatoes out of their gardens.

The first recorded instance of potatoes as a garden crop in the north dates from 1673, at Swarthmore Hall, Lancs. But by then potatoes were already being cultivated as a field crop: and in 1686 a vicar of Croston in the same county successfully sued thirteen of his parishioners for a total of £8 in tithes – multiply by between fifteen and twenty to get the sum in modern terms – on their potato crops: this means, of course, that potatoes were a cash-crop.[44] There is no need to give the evidence, but it is abundant that potatoes had become familiar in the fields and on the tables of Lancashire by 1680; it has even been claimed that they were as popular there as in Ireland. Now in this respect Lancashire was at least a century ahead of the rest of England. And since cottagers will always try to grow in their own gardens any vegetable which they have tried, liked and become used to, once their initial prejudice against anything new has been overcome, we can quite safely assume that it was in the cottage gardens of Lancashire that the potato first got a footing among the poor. Why should this have been so? Why should the Lancashire cottagers be so much readier to accept a novelty than those of southern and eastern England? For the very opposite reason to that which made the Irish do so. As Salaman points out:

It was because the worker [in Lancs.], relatively the best paid and best fed in England, had both the opportunity and the leisure to cultivate his own land in such a manner as to lend itself best to the support of himself and his family. The potato used in this manner allowed the worker greater freedom to purchase more expensive foods.

It may be so: but I think that there was another reason; the Lancashire worker was an industrial worker: it has been shown time and again that an industrial proletariat is far more intelligent, far more ready and anxious to get an education, to read books; far quicker to throw off old super-stitions and prejudices, than a peasantry.

At all events, in Lancashire the potato became the cottage gardener's favourite crop for reasons quite opposite from those which had endeared it to the Irish peasant. And at the end of the century, and even thereafter, the cottage gardens of Lancashire were the only ones in England where the potato had become king. Yet what finally persuaded the rest of the English poor to accept it at last was not the relative affluence of the Lancashire worker; it was want.

English Cottage Gardens

In the eighteenth century there were very big differences in the quality of the labourer's cottage in various parts of the country. In the Home Counties they were usually built of brick or beam and plaster, and were substantial and decent enough, if too small. Elsewhere, on the estates of improving landlords, animated more by the wish to have everything neat and seemly about them than by concern for their people's comfort, they might house their poor well, even building whole villages of stone houses: both Capability Brown and Humphry Repton were, from time to time, required to build 'model' villages for rehousing the labouring poor, notably when they had advised that the existing village spoilt the view. But outside this favoured region of the Home Counties, and excepting for a few other favoured spots, many labourers' cottages were still built of mud or dry-stone walling, and even late in the century after Arthur Young was able to make good his claim that 'cottages are perhaps one of the greatest disgraces to this country that remains to be found in it'.[45]

But, good or bad, there were cottages for every poor man, at least at the beginning of the century; the best of them were well built and had two bedrooms, one sitting-room, a hearth and chimney (taxed), and glazed windows. But what most concerns us here is that to each cottage was still attached some land for a garden. The amount of land varied: it had

Preceding pages The exuberant hedge in front of these two isolated cottages near DEPTFORD on the Wiltshire Downs contrasts with the neat vegetable plots which are clearly the cottagers' major interest.
This page The displays in the little front gardens at TENTERDEN, KENT, can be shared by every passer-by. Privacy is not generally among the amenities of the cottage garden.

Potatoes and the Cottager

declined more or less everywhere from the four acres of Elizabethan times; and it might, as in Ireland, be as little as half an acre. Not until the Enclosures movement really got under weigh and the improvers began to create the English rural scene which we have been familiar with in our own life-time and which is now, once again, being transformed, did the poor man lose that measure of independence which is conferred by the right to cultivate a garden large enough to make a serious contribution to the family table.

At the beginning of the century this piece of land was used to grow a little corn—the kind of corn depended on the locality—cabbages, turnips, parsnips, carrots, onions, beans and the same aromatic herbs and few flowers as had long been usual in small gardens. In a few cottage gardens there were some of the new exotic flowers. And most of them had from one to three or four fruit trees, perhaps some raspberry canes, perhaps a bed of strawberries, and some gooseberry and currant bushes. But, by and large, outside Lancashire, still no potatoes. Wales and the Scottish Highlands should be excluded from this statement; potatoes had become as popular there as in Lancashire, and in the west generally they were less neglected than in the south, or than in the east, where they remained virtually unknown.

A part of the reason for the slow progress which the potato was making in cottage gardens may have been that at the beginning of the century, and for most of the first half of it, food in England was very plentiful and very cheap, so that while the poor in general did not have the Lancashire workers' wage and independence, no man went hungry:

As an example of the fare of the poorest stratum of society, the dietaries of the various workhouses are instructive. In 1714 the Bristol Workhouse fed their inmates three times a day on the highest quality of food—meat, green vegetables, turnips and potatoes, and the best beer obtainable; the average cost was only 16d per week for each girl of the one hundred in the house. Another account from a Bedfordshire Workhouse in the early part of the century included meat six times a week, wheaten bread and cheese for supper every day, to which should be added milk from cows fed on the common, and the bacon from pigs which were fed on the 'wash and dregs' from the house.[46]

We are not here concerned with the potato as a field crop—in those days still the 'open-field' in most places; but it should be noted that there, too, resistance to the potato in the south and east remained just as firm. One difficulty was that if the advice of agronomists had been taken, and the fallows in the open-field system of rotation ploughed and planted with potatoes, the cottager would lose his grazing rights and would have to be compensated for them. And the resistance, in both farm and garden, went on for all the first quarter of the century, for Defoe does not even mention the potato in his *Tour of England* (1724). Here and there it was grown as a food for pigs, but there were experts who declared it useless even for that purpose. This is all the more curious in that market gardeners were growing more and more potatoes for urban markets: Phillip Miller, of *Gardener's Dictionary* fame, says that the quantity cultivated around London exceeded that of any other place in Europe. Yet Gilbert White, who, having experimented with potatoes in his own garden from 1758, actually offered the cottagers of his parish cash premiums to plant them, failed to convince them that potatoes were worth a place in their gardens.[47]

By the end of the first quarter of the eighteenth century the majority of the English cottagers were eating white, wheaten bread as a staple: the quantity of other grains used in the flour had steadily declined as the price of wheat fell. This wheaten loaf became more and more important–disproportionately so–as more common land was enclosed and the cottagers lost poultry, cows–and therefore milk–and even some of their pigs. Yet still, in the mid 1760s, when Arthur Young made the first of his three tours of England,[48] he found no potatoes being grown in Home Counties cottage gardens; the same was true in the Midlands and the east. But in the north the practice of growing them in cottage gardens had spread from Lancashire; Young found them in most small gardens in the North and West Ridings of Yorkshire, Cumberland and Northumberland;[49] he only touched on Wales, but there too the potato was well established in the poor man's garden.

But in the third quarter of the century certain political events and technological advances brought to an end a period of relative prosperity for the working poor: in September 1767 the American colonists began that boycott of British imports, in protest against taxation without representation, which led a few years later to the War of Independence. As a result, the English hosiers lost their best overseas market and there was widespread unemployment. In 1764 James Hargreaves had perfected the spinning-jenny, and five years later Arkwright perfected his spinning machine: many cotton spinners were thrown out of work; in 1775 Watt perfected the steam engine, thus providing a source of power for new

Potatoes and the Cottager

factories. The cottager's industry-plus-garden economy was being swiftly destroyed. Country cottagers moved off the land into towns where there might be work in factories. The price of wheat began to climb; but wages did not rise. By then the commoners of England had also lost their commons. Between many thousands of cottagers and starvation there was little, sometimes nothing, but their gardens.

Those were the conditions which enabled the potato at last to complete its conquest of the English cottage garden. And by the end of the century that conquest was complete everywhere excepting in Norfolk and Suffolk. When Coke of Holkham, the great agricultural improver, after five years of experimental cultivation of potatoes which made him an expert on the crop, urged them on his tenants, their answer was that 'perhaps t'wouldn't poison the pigs'. But at last even the cottagers of those two recalcitrant counties gave up their obstinate prejudices; and after two centuries of struggle, the potato became king of the small man's garden throughout all the land.

The concrete squirrel and the trumpeting elephant, the wheel gate, the bell and the pebble-encrusted piers at CHURCH STRETTON, SHROPSHIRE, are all fruits of the cult of the Picturesque in its last lamentable stages.

[6]
A Museum
of Plants

For nearly two hundred years, from the beginning of the seventeenth until the end of the eighteenth century, the cottage garden changed hardly at all. There was no reason why it should: for it was the poor man's garden, and the history of the poor man's garden and the history of the poor, until the technological revolution, in all countries and at all times was that it had no history: for 4,000 years the Egyptian *fellah* has toiled at the *shadouf*; he is still doing so, and I take him to be a suitable symbol for the poor everywhere. The rise of one nation and the fall of another, political adventures, discovery in the sciences, joy in the arts, the profits of industry and the advances in the comforts and decencies of living were, until recently, for a small élite class; only now is the majority beginning to get its share of both material and cultural wealth. It is grimly significant that the one great change in the cottage garden in the period under review was the introduction, which we have just discussed, of the potato; an introduction due, in all but a few favoured places where the poor were just beginning to get a few crumbs of the industrial cake, not to a betterment in the cottager's conditions, but to the threat of starvation.

But if the cottage garden remained very much what it had long been, in the long run it could not fail to be affected, belatedly as I have said, by some of the changes in great gardens; moreover we have to include under the general heading 'cottage garden' the small suburban garden which was soon, once again, to become important. It will therefore be best to review the major changes in the period 1600 to 1800, pointing out from time to time those which were of significance for the small garden.

Of these by far the most considerable was the continuous enrichment of the garden flora. That enrichment is to be found reflected in the difference between the plant lists in Parkinson's *Paradisi* and John Rea's *Flores, Ceres and*

Pomona. Half a century separates these two books; Rea, in his introduction, says that having considered what he calls 'Mr Parkinson's garden of pleasant flowers', and compared his own collections with what he found there, he,

. . . easily perceived his book to want the addition of many noble things of new choicing, and that a multitude of these there set out were by time grown stale and for unworthiness turned out of every good garden.[50]

But that unworthiness was not as apparent to the cottager as to Mr Rea and his friends; and had it been, the cottager could not have afforded to dispense with what he had. Old cultivars, in short, lingered much longer, often more than a century longer and occasionally for several centuries longer, in the cottage gardens than in the gardens of the prosperous burgesses or of the rich. The fact is that the cottage gardener, if only by his want of means, did a public service by preserving, for later generations who might again appreciate them, old garden plants banished from the great gardens and the gardens of the middle class by Mr Rea's 'new choicings', and still newer choicings of men who came after Rea. There are some known cases of such unwitting conservation: certain forms of sweet william, the simpler pinks, many kinds of double and coloured primroses, the gold-laced polyanthus, the old ranunculas cultivars.[51] It is a fact that it was from cottage gardens that these and many plants valued in our own time were recovered. To that list one could add many others which, having been dismissed from the great garden for their offensive simplicity during the nineteenth century, were restored to the favour of people of taste by such great gardeners as Victoria Sackville-West. Some of the old shrub roses, for example, survived only in cottage gardens until rescued a few decades ago.

Furthermore, the cottage garden has sometimes acted as a 'gene pool' for plant breeding material whose value was only realized comparatively recently: Roy Genders quotes the case of the J. W. Unwin sweet peas, found in a Histon (Cambridgeshire) cottage garden; of the East Lothian strain of stocks, preserved in the cottage gardens of a small neighbourhood since Tudor times; of the Fenbow 'nutmeg clove' carnation, preserved in a single cottage garden since 1652; of Mr Montagu Allwood's discovery of the ancestor of the '*Allwoodii*' pinks in another cottage garden; these are only some of the cases quoted by that author.[52] And there is the now familiar tale of the discovery of the miniature roses, or rather the proto-miniature roses, in the window-boxes of a Swiss village.

But, considering the period 1600 to 1800, the point is, of course, that the plants and genes thus preserved to us were not then cottage garden plants, or not for the most part. Today's cottage garden plant has always been yesterday's fashionable plant, and, as I have said, the cottage garden flora tends to reflect the great garden flora of the previous age of gardening or the previous age but one. Not so much the cottager's conservatism as his poverty has thus made him the curator of a museum of ancient plants. And, as it happened, plants which were pushed out of the grand garden into the cottage garden were often better, because simpler, more 'natural', less coarsened by too much hybridization aimed to produce great size or gaudy colour, than the plants which replaced them: for it is fashion, more than anything else, which displaces one cultivar by a newer one, and novelty alone is, in the eye of the rich enthusiast, a virtue. The poor enthusiast's taste is no better; but he cannot afford to indulge it; and so he preserves the unfashionable plants.

So the great changes which took place in the period we are here concerned with were only reflected very belatedly in the cottage garden, and for the most part not at all. For one thing, the scale was wrong.

During the Commonwealth period the principal changes were in economic gardening, both in private kitchen gardens and in market gardens. Such changes have always been far more important to the cottager than changes in ornamental gardening. I have already referred to Hartlib's *Legacie of Husbandry;* Hartlib was a Pole who settled in England during the reign of Charles I and who was given a pension of £100 a year by Oliver Cromwell. Among his other recommendations, he urges much more planting of fruit in English gardens and orchards. Fruit and vegetable gardens are, he says,

. . . a wonderful improver of lands, as it plainly appears by this, that they give extraordinary rates for land, from 40 shillings per acre to 9 pound and dig and howe and dung their lands which costeth very much . . . yet I know divers which by two or three acres of land maintain themselves and family. . . .

And he complains:

We have not nurseries sufficient in this land of Apples, Pears, Cherries, Vines, Chestnuts, Almonds etc: but gentlemen are necessitated to send to London some 100 miles for them.

As a consequence of the writings–and often more practical work–of men like Hartlib, fruit and vegetable growing did improve in England. Ralph Austen, another great advocate of market garden progress, managed to combine

Brick paths such as that at MEOPHAM, KENT, are conspicuous features of cottage gardens on the Kentish clay.

A Museum of Plants

in his writings on the subject sound horticultural science with Puritan religious feeling in some extraordinary works in which, for example, every process in the management of fruit trees is compared with a stage in the Christian's progress through life.[53] Yet Austen's work was particularly valuable in helping to rid horticulture of superstitious practices. It is not, perhaps, surprising that such practices lingered longer in the cottage garden than in the great garden, just as the older cultivars of both economic and ornamental plants did: for the errors were not of the old witch kind, the importance of moon phases and planetary conjunction; they were pseudo-scientific. Austen tells his readers that it is not true that if you engrave an inscription on a peach stone and then plant the stone, the resulting peach tree will bear fruit with the inscription on all the stones; nor that fruit can be given a special flavour by soaking the seed its tree is to be grown from in a liquor with that flavour; nor that scions of apple soaked in pike's blood will ultimately bring forth only red fruit. He advises that fruit trees be moved early rather than late in the autumn, or in the spring; and that they be planted at least ten yards apart, instead of being crowded, as was the common practice.

Austen did another great service by actually naming some of the books which were responsible for spreading nonsensical ideas on how to cultivate a garden – Gabriel Platt's *Country Farm*, for example, and the works of the famous 'Didymus' Hill. Cottage gardeners were the last to be edified by sound teaching such as Austen's; but edified, in the long run, they were, and slowly absurd practices disappeared and sound horticulture became the rule even at the lowest social level.

Austen's lists of good fruit varieties show that change was continuous, although some of the older kinds of fruit still appear: if his 'Gilloflour' apple is the Cornish gillyflower, it was a newcomer to the rest of England. He names varieties of peach and apricot as well as apples, plums and pears. He knows, he says, only one variety of figs which can be relied on to ripen in England, the 'great Blew fig, as large as a Catharine pear . . .'. But it needs a wall.

An unexpected way in which the Civil War did gardening a good service was by forcing Sir Thomas Hanmer, an ardent Cavalier, out of public life and into his garden, to pass the time throughout the period of the Commonwealth. Hanmer was a born gardener, if there is such a thing; his garden notebook had been known to specialists for centuries before it was actually published, as *The Garden Book of Sir*

The homely cottage garden at LOUGHRIGG TARN in the Lake District introduces an even more reassuringly human note into the wide expanse of water, wood and rock than the landscaped meadows on the far side of the lake.

Thomas Hanmer, in 1933. He describes changes in garden design: vistas are being opened; clipped rosemary or privet edging to flower beds is disappearing; French parterres are in fashion, and likewise the French fashion for clipped evergreens planted at regular intervals. Hanmer gives us the dimensions of typical gardens: a nobleman's garden is about 300 yards by 200; a gentleman's, 80 yards by 60. The cottager might sometimes have as much land as a gentleman; but, of course, most of it was used for staples like beans, a bit of corn, and later potatoes; the ornamental part was very small, confined to the immediate neighbourhood of the cottage.

But if the new fashion in garden design could in no way concern the cottager, Hanmer's flowers were not excluded from the cottage garden: there were a score of ways in which a new bulb, a cutting, a bit of root of plants from the great house garden got into the cottager's hands. Hanmer gives primacy to tulips; he grew fifty-six kinds, some blooming from as early as March, others well into the summer. He grows auriculas, anemones, primroses and cowslips in great variety: it is among such genera that are to be found some of the beautiful old garden varieties which survived into our own age only in some cottage gardens. Hanmer had a 'winter-house'–a substantial shed glazed on the south side only, in which he could overwinter tender evergreens, and grow those *Amaryllis* which he called Indian narcissus. He knew, and grew, twenty-one varieties of rose; most of them seem to have been gallicas or damasks, but one is probably *Rosa haemispherica*; at all events, it had yellow flowers. Hanmer also gave a great deal of attention to evergreens, including the newly introduced cedar of Lebanon, and oranges, which had to be moved into the winter-house during the cold weather, and which were grown chiefly for their fragrant flowers, although they could be grown for their fruit, as some were, and likewise lemons, at least as early as Charles I's reign. It is surprising to discover that, as early as Hanmer's day, English gardeners were growing *Erythrinas* from Brazil, *Schinus* from Peru, pineapples from Mexico, and other rare exotics from very remote countries: these were never, of course, of any interest to the cottage gardener.

Another man who did much to advance the science of horticulture, as well as arboriculture, at this time was John Evelyn; I have described how his colleagues in the Royal Society asked him to include in his *Sylva* a chapter on the cultivation of potatoes. One of his most useful services was that of pointing out that some of the new evergreens which were being treated as tender and taking up precious space in the winter-house were, in fact, hardy plants–*Phillyrea*, for example. Not until our own day could the cottage gardener share the richer man's pleasure of growing tropical and sub-tropical plants; so that a whole range of beautiful plants were impossible for the poor man. But he also lost plants which he might well have grown because time and again new introductions were regarded as tender when in fact they were hardy. A good example of this is to be found in the English garden career of *Camellia japonica*; hardy down to zero Fahrenheit and even lower, it was for so long grown, as tender, under glass, that only now is it appearing in cottage gardens, excepting in Cornwall where, because of the work done on the species by J. C. Williams of Caerhays, its hardiness was early realized; in that country there are magnificent old camellia bushes in cottage gardens. Finally, on the subject of Evelyn's services to gardening, he published what was perhaps the first popular month-by-month gardening guide.[54]

Like Hanmer, John Rea, whose *Flora, Ceres and Pomona* I have already referred to, gave primacy to tulips as garden flowers, and described how to plant the several different classes of tulip. He grew daffodils and other narcissi, auriculas, of course, many sorts of iris, some of which he raised from seed, hyacinths, alliums, peonies, over a score of crocus varieties, colchiums, anemones in variety, ranunculas yuccas, wall-flowers, a great variety of primulas, stocks, carnations, lychnis, pinks, mallows, delphiniums, scabious, perennial sweet peas (not, not yet, the annuals), cornflowers, lupins, most of the aromatic herbs, and, also as an ornamental, tomatoes. Finally, Rea grew a great variety of all kinds of fruit. It will be obvious from this list that it was in the late seventeenth century that a great many of what we think of as 'cottage garden flowers' first became common in English gardens.

Having named the tomato as growing in Rea's garden, as it was in a few other English gardens at the time, this will be as good a place as any to say something about the extraordinary career of a fruit plant which has been more valuable to the cottage gardener than any fruit introduced since Roman times; which has become a staple of the poor man's diet; which has contributed as much to his health and pleasure as any garden plant I can think of. The tomato took three centuries to travel from the Aztec market-gardens into the English cottage gardens; and in England, starting as a florist's curiosity in 1670, it has become, three centuries later, gastronomically and economically an even more important fruit than the apple.

The story begins in the mountain region of Peru–Bolivia–Ecuador,[55] where the plant is found wild, and where it was presumably domesticated by gardeners of the pre-Inca societies of that region. It spread south through the lands and nations of the Inca Empire, and also, somehow, made its way into the gardens of Aztec Mexico. Doubtless it was grown on the famous floating island market gardens which served the great markets of the lake city of Tenochtitlan. Although the original provenance of the plant seems to be realized in one of the earlist Eurpean names for it–*Mala peruviana*[56]–it seems clear that we had the tomato by way of Mexico, for our name for it is a corruption of an Aztec word, *tumatl*.

The seeds which first reached Europe were not those of a wild plant, but of an ancient garden plant.[57] Like the haricot beans and 'sweet' peppers, it was a staple crop in Mexican gardens.[58] It is not clear where it was first grown in Europe; it may have been tried in the Canary Islands and introduced from there into Spain. But it was first noticed in Italy, in 1554, by Matthioli. That great botanist must, for some reason, have believed the fruit to be poisonous, or at least unwholesome, and consequently called it *Mala insana*. If he recognized its kinship with the Old World *Solanaceae* he probably thought it wise to be cautious, for most of them are poisonous. Despite this evil name, confirmed in Tournefort's renaming of it, *Lycopersicum*, 'wolf-peach', the tomato was being quite widely grown and readily eaten in Italy in the latter part of the sixteenth century.

In the north, however, either because of its bad name, or because it was more difficult to ripen, the new plant made very slow progress. Thus, a century after Matthioli's first notice of it, the tomato was being libelled by the French horticulturist and botanist, Dalechamps:

Ces pommes, comme aussi toute la plante, refrodisent toutefois moins que le mandragore; parquoy il est dangereux d'en user. Toutefois aucuns mangent les pommes cuite, avec huile, sel et poivre. Elles donnent peu de nourriture au corps, laquelle est mauvaise et corrumpue.

(*These apples, and likewise all the plant, chill the body albeit less than mandrake; wherefore, it is dangerous to eat them. Yet some do so, cooked, with oil, salt and pepper. They give little nourishment to the body, and that little bad and rotten.*)

But then, of course, Dalechamps had not had the advantage of having heard of Vitamin c.

LOWER BRAILES, WARWICKSHIRE Lilac, introduced into England in Tudor times, reached the cottage garden in the Jacobean period. The older kinds are most likely to be found in cottage gardens.

A Museum of Plants

Pommes, apples: the word was often used, as in Greek, to mean, simply, fruits. But in the north—and only in the north, which is curious—tomatoes got a name as an aphrodisiac, whence the vernacular names of *pommes d'amour* and, in English, love-apples. Tomatoes were still appearing under that name in Vilmorin-Andrieux's seed catalogue for 1760; and still being listed with the ornamentals. It was not really until the second quarter of the nineteenth century that the value of the tomato as a food began to be realized; it was in 1830, for example, that in both England and America breeding of better garden kinds was started. How long after that did this valuable plant get into the English cottage garden? Not, certainly, until our own century, and not effectively until well after the First World War. In the 1880s Flora Thompson, living in an Oxfordshire village, saw tomatoes for the first time in the pack of an itinerant pedlar whose ordinary wares were oranges and lemons: he told her:

Love-apples, me dear, love-apples they be; though some ignorant folks be calling them tommytoes. But you don't want any of they-nasty sour things they be, as only the gentry eat.[59]

So, then, the plant, which is now almost a must in every cottage garden, every allotment, and every small greenhouse, and which was first being cultivated by north Italians before the first Elizabeth came to the throne, did not really establish itself in our own small gardens until well over three centuries later.

Turning, again, to the ornamentals: lilies, from both Europe and from North America, now became much commoner in our gardens. As we have seen, the madonna lily had long been a commonplace (though not in cottage gardens at first), and the martagon had long since been introduced. But now there were others. Gerard records the introduction of one, *Lilium chalcedonicum*, from Constantinople.

. . . it was sent among many other bulbs of rare and daintie flowers by Master Harbran ambassador there, unto my honourable good lord and master the Lord Treasurer of England, who bestowed it upon me for my garden.

Hanmer refers to a 'single deep red or Bloody lily', perhaps *L. bulbiferum*, a common European lily. That, rather than *L. canadense rubrum* (see Alicia Amherst) must have been the lily also referred to by Gilbert in his *Florists' Vade Mecum* as '. . . a flower so vulgar, every countrywoman can form an idea of it in a stranger's head . . .' In short, it was in the cottage gardens. Still, *L. canadense* had probably been introduced by then; Hanmer describes something like it and calls it 'Lily of Canada or the West Indies'. Again, going by

The rhododendron bushes in this garden at ST MARY'S, SCILLY ISLES, suggest their locality for the rhododendron was never a cottage garden plant except in Cornwall and the Scillies. Another plant found in old cottage gardens of this region is also seen growing here – the smaller variety of gladiola.

[75]

descriptions, Hanmer had two other new introductions: *L. pomponium* and *L. superbum*. Of these, and all the lilies since introduced, only the common *martagon*, *bulbiferum* and later *L. regale* ever competed seriously with the madonna lily in cottagers' gardens.

The principal foreign influences on the English garden during the Restoration were French and Dutch, but particularly French. There is no evidence that the great Le Nôtre ever came to England, although many garden historians claim that he did; even more say that de la Quintineye, his horticultural collaborator, visited this country; I can find no evidence for that either. But John Rose, Charles II's gardener, studied under him in Paris, or at least under Vespasian Robin at the Jardin des Plantes; and both Evelyn and the nurserymen London and Wise translated his textbook on fruit-growing. Some other well-known French garden designers, notably the brothers Mollet, certainly did work in England. But theirs was not the kind of influence to make any impression on the cottage garden – elaborate or even simple *parterres*, multiple fountains, cascades and fanciful waterworks, plantations of trees in serried military ranks, such things as these were hardly for the cottager.

On the other hand, he might find a use for the latest techniques in garden pest control; he might try to rid his garden of moles with some such receipt as:

Take red herrings and cutting them in pieces, burn the pieces on the molehills, or you may put garlicks or leeks in the mouth of the Hill, and the moles will leave the ground.[60]

Caterpillars were dealt with by lighting smudge fires, although some authorities thought that the unnatural heat of the smoke was bad for the trees; it was safer to pick the creatures off by hand. Small birds, such as bullfinches, then as now a serious pest in gardens, especially fruit gardens, were shot with a 'stone-bow' or a 'peece'.

Of the many men who advanced the art and science of gardening in England from the seventeenth to the eighteenth century, few were as effective as London and Wise. There were, and long had been, other successful nurserymen, and we shall come to one of them presently, but these two were the prototypes of the modern nurserymen. It is true that, on the whole, cottage gardeners did not yet *buy* their plants; but the new, rising middle class began to do so. Our gardens have depended on such nurserymen, since London and Wise set a pattern, for the enrichment of their flora. In their own additions to their translations of French textbooks – *The Compleat*

Preceding pages The sparkling flint walls of Victoria Place, ERISWELL, SUFFOLK, set off the cottage gardens with their miniature box hedges, dahlias, michaelmas daisies and the garter grass which flourishes in sandy soils.

Gardener (from de la Quintineye); *The Retired Gardener* (from Louis Liger); and *The Solitary Gardener* (from Le Gentil), these nurserymen initiated the practice of giving brief and clear instructions which modern nurserymen use in their catalogues today. They did this in the form of dialogues between the customer and themselves. They also gave the best ways of propagating the common garden flowers.

Towards the end of the seventeenth century and the beginning of the eighteenth, there were advances in greenhouse design and building. Hothouses were needed for the raising and display of the very large number of tropical exotics which were reaching England from all over the world. The small gardener of today, with his automated small hothouse or greenhouse, owes it to such seventeenth-century pioneers as John Evelyn who, after consultation with Robert Hooke, another Fellow of the Royal Society, and Sir Christopher Wren, published a design for a heated greenhouse. It was scientifically designed to maintain a constant change and circulation of air which was drawn through a complex of earthenware pipes heated outside the house.

Another advance, made early in the eighteenth century, was in the deliberate hybridization of garden plants. The Dutch tulip breeders were, no doubt, the pioneers, but one Englishman in this field was also an innovator in another aspect of gardening. Thomas Fairchild (1667–1729) was one of several nurserymen who had their gardens at Hoxton, outside London. He seems to have been the first gardener to try to produce new garden *Dianthus* cultivars by crossing sweet william with carnation. Fairchild also turned his attention particularly to the problems of the urban gardener, and in 1722 he published a book especially for the town gardener, *The City Garden*, in which he dealt, among many other things, with the question of air pollution affecting garden plants. For example, he gives a list of evergreens which will thrive best in London gardens, 'as everything will not prosper because of the smoke of the sea-coal'. So that problem is also older than we are apt to think.

From the point of view of the small gardener – cottager, townsman, or suburbanite – probably the greatest teacher of gardening in the early eighteenth century was Philip Miller. It is true that his books were intended for the country gentleman, but the wealth of sound gardening information which they contained formed a body of lore which lingered on among cottage and suburban gardeners long after the professionals and the gentry had turned to newer pundits.

English Cottage Gardens

Miller was the London-born son of a Scottish market-gardener. He started on his own as a 'florist', that is a nurseryman, and he taught himself horticulture and botany to such effect that Sir Hans Sloane had him appointed supervisor of the Chelsea Physic Garden which he had started and endowed. That was in 1722, and twelve years later this garden, under Miller's management, had become so famous among gardeners and botanists all over Europe that even Linnaeus came to see it–and, incidentally, to persuade Miller to adopt the Linnaean system of plant classification, which he did: for although he was a self-educated (and self-opinionated) empiricist, Miller was one of nature's scientists. He published two books of the greatest value to both professional and amateur gardeners: *The Gardener and Florist's Dictionary, or a Complete System of Horticulture* in 1724; and *The Gardeners' Dictionary* in 1731.

By the middle of the eighteenth century, kitchen gardening in England–in the cottage gardens as well as the market gardens and the gardens of the great houses–had made very great progress. Then, as formerly and thereafter, it was in vegetables that the cottage gardener was chiefly interested. Improved varieties of cabbages and cauliflowers, beans, haricots, leeks, lettuce, spinach and radishes were widely available. And there were more and better varieties of fruit than ever before.

The second half of the eighteenth century was the great age of the English picturesque landscape garden, an age dominated by three artists–William Kent, Lancelot (Capability) Brown, and Humphry Repton. There is no point in telling the story of that remarkable revolution in taste here,[61] for obviously it could have little or no effect on the shape of the cottage garden. Indeed, never was the barrier of wealth excluding the majority of Englishmen from taking any part in the 'cultural' life of their own country as grimly insurmountable as it was between 1750 and 1800. It was perhaps during that half-century that the cottage garden began to become a sort of museum for the old garden flowers, as the landscape garden artists swept out of existence hundreds of old gardens, with their stock of garden plants which had been novelties between 1600 and 1700.

A few cottage gardens benefited, at least in their flora, from the fact that a small number of improving landlords extended their operations to include even the labourers' cottages. But this had no significance for the cottage garden in general.

A Museum of Plants

Nothing makes the vast gulf which separated the cottager's from the gentleman's garden clearer than the design of one cottage garden made by one landscape garden artist. This was the garden which Humphry Repton, creator of a hundred grand gardens all over England and Wales and architect of many a great house, made for himself at Hare Street, Essex, and in which he spent many long days in his wheel chair after being crippled in a carriage accident. This little garden is described, and illustrated with his water-colour drawings, in the last of his three major books.[62] It is a garden in the middle of a village–Repton had to use his knowledge and skill to obscure the sight, from his front door, of the village butcher's shop; there are lawns, some specimen trees, groups of flowering shrubs planted to create a miniature vista, a single bed of herbaceous perennial flowers. Where are the beans and cabbages? Nowhere, or out of sight. In short, Repton's cottage garden is a gentleman's landscape garden *in petto;* its like was rarely to be seen again until, in the mid twentieth century, middle class townsmen began to buy workers' cottages, in both country and town; and to make cottage gardens which bore, to those of the past 1,000 years, the same relation as Marie Antionette's dairy to a real one.

The lighthouse placed with such precision between the windows of this cottage at LOSTWITHIEL, CORNWALL, is a last degenerate descendant of the folly erected on an 18th-century gentleman's estate.

[7]
Rural
and
Suburban

At the beginning of the nineteenth century the country cottage garden still lay deep in the pre-industrial world, although the Industrial Revolution was by then under weigh. At the same time there was something new in the towns: a new kind of small suburban garden, to become the pattern for millions of them in the next hundred years, and very different from the country cottage garden. The little garden of the new Londoner or Mancunian or Bristolian was shaped and planted for pleasure; the country cottage garden was, as it always had been, shaped by need, and as the century progressed and the countryman became poorer, that need was as sharp as it had ever been. I shall try to give some examples of both kinds of garden. In the country case there are some curious differences between the cottage gardens of the declining class of fairly prosperous cottager, survivals from the late eighteenth and early years of the nineteenth century; and those of the new and increasingly large number of rural poor, people living on a wage of 10s a week in a world of rising prices.

In a typical Home Counties or South or West Midlands neighbourhood there were two kinds of cottages: the survivals, with some kind of beam-and-plaster construction, outside walls whitewashed, roof thatched, diamond-paned windows; and, much more common, the newer brick or stone boxes with slate roofs. The best country cottages had two bedrooms; most had only one, which had to be divided by a screen or curtain–parents on one side, children on the other. But all these cottages had a garden.

Some of the older type of cottages, with relatively large gardens, almost small-holdings, survived until the end of the century. Flora Thompson describes one such place, in an Oxfordshire hamlet, in the 1880s, but it should be taken as an example of a kind of cottage and garden which really belongs to much earlier in the century. It was a long, low,

A diminished, sentimental relative at DUDDENHOE END, ESSEX, of the sculptured goddesses of the great Georgian landscape gardens.
Right It was at least two centuries after its introduction in the seventeenth century before the cottager grew clematis, but the montana framing this door at UGGESHALL, SUFFOLK, looks completely at home.

[82]

thatched building with whitewashed walls and diamond-paned windows. It had a porch made of 'rustic'-work–shortly to be deliberately copied in the suburban gardens, but about the only feature that was–overgrown with honeysuckle, a honeysuckle which would have been dug out of a hedgerow.

Excepting the inn it was the largest house in the hamlet, and of its two downstairs rooms, one was used as a kind of kitchen store-room, with pots and pans and a big red crockery water vessel at one end, and potatoes in sacks, and beans and peas laid out to dry at the other. The apple crop was stored on racks suspended beneath the ceiling and bunches of herbs dangled below. In one corner stood the big brewing copper in which old Sally still brewed with good malt and hops once a quarter. . . . [63]

The garden of this cottage was a large one, and at the bottom of it was a small field where Dick, the cottager, old Sally's husband, grew a crop of corn; this would have been either wheat or barley; and, had it been in the north country, oats. Nearer to the cottage itself there were fruit trees. The flower garden and the bee-hives were shielded from the cold quarters by a dense, clipped yew hedge; one reason why the cottager early took to topiary–at least of this simple rect-angular kind–was that it is better as a wind-shield than any wall. A yew hedge of this kind will filter a gale to a zephyr; put a wall in its place, and the wind simply leaps over it and strikes as hard as ever beyond what is called the wind-shadow.

The flower garden inside the shelter of this yew hedge was tended by old Sally; the vegetable garden outside it, by her husband. The flower garden contained a small collection of roses–Seven Sisters, Maiden's Blush, moss rose, monthly rose, cabbage rose, blood rose, and a 'York and Lancaster'–that pied white and red rose which in our own time has been rescued from the cottage garden refuge and again widely planted. Groundlings included lavender, pinks, wall-flowers, sweet william and a number of varieties of tulip. Note that the cottager and his wife were eighty years old, so that they had been born about 1800. They remembered a time, when they were children, when country people were not so poor as their own neighbours now were. Old Sally's father had had not only such a garden as she and her husband still had, but also pigs, chickens, geese and a cow; for he had had commoner's rights. The new poverty was reflected in the fact that other houses like theirs had been divided into two to accommodate two families instead of one; and the gardens were proportionately smaller. And such household goods,

A perfect example of the cottage garden at KERSEY, SUFFOLK.

The cottager's back garden is traditionally given over to vegetables but in the front space he lets himself go, perhaps on roses, delphiniums and larkspurs as at SLAUGHAM, SUSSEX (*above*) or on the formality of clipped box as at BURNHAM OVERY, NORFOLK (*below*).

like decently made furniture, or clocks, as her neighbours
had, were all heirlooms, a relic of the time when all the
hamlet women were lacemakers and got good money for their
work, money which, since they lived well enough off their
gardens and commons, was for spending in the market town.

Such was the cottage garden at the beginning of the
nineteenth century.

In the first half of the century three forces were at work to
produce a new kind of small garden: John Claudius Loudon;
the new horticultural press; and horticultural societies. In
this chapter we are concerned only with the first of the three.
Loudon and his wife can fairly be said to have created the
nineteen-century suburban garden which, in the long run,
influenced the shape and planting of the country cottage
garden too.

Loudon was born, the son of a small Lanarkshire farmer,
in 1773. He had a simple, conventional schooling, and at the
age of fourteen he was apprenticed to an Edinburgh nursery
firm. While he was working there, learning the gardening
trade, he studied botany and taught himself to be a very
good draughtsman; at the same time he employed teachers
to teach him French and Italian, earning the money to pay
their fees by doing translation from those languages for an
Edinburgh publisher. His power of learning was extraordinary and was in part due to astonishing application; for
example, on two nights of every week he denied himself
sleep altogether, and worked at his books through the night.
It is at least possible that this contributed to the precarious
state of his health during the rest of his life.

In 1803, when he was twenty, Loudon went to London
and found employment with landscape gardeners and nurserymen, and at the age of twenty-three was elected a
Fellow of the Linnaean Society. His first published work,
a paper on the laying out and planting of London squares,
belongs to this part of his life. But in 1806 he was stricken
down with rheumatic fever, and for the next two years he
was an invalid. However, he published a paper on English
farming, and in 1809, probably with some backing from his
father, he took Tew Park Farm in Oxfordshire and made it
into a school for aspiring young farmers; he did this because
he had realized that English farming was lagging behind
Lanarkshire farming and that he had much to teach. This
venture was remarkably successful, and in 1812 he found
that he had £15,000 in hand. He shut up shop, invested the
money, and went off to travel all over northern Europe,

getting as far as Moscow in the wake of Napoleon's army. But the undertakings in which he had invested his fortune failed, and he returned to England to make a living again. He became a successful horticultural journalist; but what else he did until 1819 is not clear.

In 1819, however, he was again able to go abroad, and went this time to the south of Europe; at the same time he was preparing his *Encyclopaedia of Gardening*. Some time in 1820 he broke his arm; it was badly set by a bungling surgeon, and for the next five years he was almost continuously in pain. To relieve this he used laudanum, became addicted to it, and after a year or so was taking it at the rate of a wine-glass full every eight hours.

Loudon's *Encyclopaedia of Gardening* was successfully published in 1822; he then set about writing an *Encyclopaedia of Agriculture*. Meanwhile he was involved in journalism, at one time being editor of no less than five monthlies at the same time, and also founding magazines of his own. His new *Encyclopaedia* was published in 1825, and in the same year it became necessary to have the arm which had been troubling him for five years amputated. He then decided to break himself of the opium habit, and by slowly and regularly reducing his dose of laudanum he did so completely.

One of the books which had been sent to him, as editor, for review was called *The Mummy*: clever and witty, it was an imaginary account of England in the twenty-second century. As a result of his review of this book, which he liked and praised perhaps because twenty-second-century farmers used steam ploughs, he met the author; he had expected to meet a mature man; the author of *The Mummy* turned out to be a girl of twenty-three, Jane Webb. Loudon, at that time forty-seven and in poor health—he always was—fell in love with her, and she with him. They married, and thereafter they worked as one for the rest of his life; after his death Jane Loudon carried on the work they had planned for the future, and so wore herself out in doing so that she herself died of exhaustion, as much as of any more specific cause.

There would be no point in our context in noticing all the Loudons' works. He founded the *Gardeners' Magazine* in 1826 and made a success of it for five years. He was active as landscape gardener, architect, botanist, publicist, journalist and author, and in 1830 he published a *Manual of Cottage Gardening*. The book with which, for its enormous influence on the new kind of small gardens—the, as it were, urban cottage garden—we are concerned with was called in its first

Gardens at FULHAM, LONDON, which owe much to the cottage style.

and early editions *The Suburban Gardener and Villa Companion*, and in its later edition, issued by Jane Loudon after her husband's death, *The Villa Gardener*. It was first published in 1838. It deals with medium-sized and large gardens of the new 'gardenesque' kind–a Loudon invention; but it also deals very thoroughly and conscientiously with the very small garden, the garden of one square perch, that is, thirty square yards.

The Loudons discuss in great detail the difficulties inherent in the fixed oblong shape of the new suburban gardens; how to overcome or minimize the disadvantages of shade cast by walls, fences and neighbouring houses; how to make the best of awkwardly shaped pieces of land. In many passages like the following he tried to do, for the little man with a very small bit of garden, what men like Capability Brown and Humphry Repton had done for the rich with their vast gardens:

If we imagine a narrow slip (say about 20 feet or 30 feet in breadth which is the general width of the gardens of the smallest suburban houses in the neighbourhood of London), placed in the direction of east and west, and that the fences are ten feet high, it is evident that the greater part of the garden will be in the shade every day of the year; and the whole of it will be under shade at least two months of every winter. On the contrary, if a plot of ground of the same width, and with fences of the same height, be placed in the direction north and south, the sun will shine on every part of it during the warmest portion of every day in the year. In the latter garden, in the climate of London, peaches and grapes might be ripened, while in the former nothing would thrive but ivy, and a few of the commoner shrubs and herbaceous plants.[64]

A clever diagram shows the effect of alignment with the eight principal points of the compass, on the exposure of a long, narrow, suburban garden. Loudon gives directions for laying down pipes and fixing stand-pipes, for drainage, for making good paths, and even for 'arrangements for posts to support clothes lines'. Here at last, then, was an expert who paid real attention to the small gardener's problems in a thoroughly practical way. And that the small urban and suburban gardener was quick to benefit from the Loudons' advice is beyond question. We owe to them a good deal of that original interest in our small gardens and the sound traditions of design and care for them, which make them the best in the world.

But we must now look again at the country cottage garden. Could Loudon help the cottager? He tried to when he wrote a manual for him in 1820, more used by the gentry reduced to living in cottages than by the many, the real cottagers; but the fact is that if, thus early in the century, there were too few readers among cottagers, later the countryman was too desperately poor to be helped in this way: the 'Hungry Forties' were just ahead. I shall return to this aspect of the matter below; but it may be said here that in the very long run the cottager did receive some of the benefit which Loudon intended for him. And even in *The Suburban Gardener* there was no aspect of gardening, even on the smallest scale, which he neglected. For instance:

In the smallest suburban houses the common substitute for a greenhouse is the window-sill; and the greatest extent to which this kind of gardening can be carried is by having the sill made to project 2ft or 3ft from the wall of the house and enclosing it with an outside bow window. Into the space between the two windows the warm air of the room may be admitted at pleasure; and if the panes of both windows are large, and kept at all times perfectly clean, the view into this plant cabinet from the interior of the room will be agreeable and create an allusion to the green-house of the villa, or the conservatory of the mansion.[64]

A small garden, but not a cottage garden, despite the inclusion of some typical cottage flowers among the exotics. For the elements of this HAMPSTEAD garden one must go not to the traditional English cottage garden but to the *Letters* of the Younger Pliny.

English Cottage Gardens

Loudon bears always in mind that his reader does not have a gardener, unless perhaps a man who comes for a few hours every week to tidy up and mow the lawn. He explains where to put the flower bed or beds in diverse conditions, how to design for the most pleasing effect when the garden is to be seen from the windows of the house. The Loudons even do their best to teach taste:

Whatever kinds of flowers may be admitted into a flowerbed or border, one principle of planting must never be lost sight of; that is distinctness, or the keeping of every particular plant perfectly isolated, and though near to, yet never allowing it to touch the adjoining plants. This is merely the principle *of the gardenesque applied to flowers; and it is so decidedly preferable in point of convenience for culture, to planting so close together as that the plants will soon join together and cover the surface of the soil, that we should never for a moment think of recommending what may be called the picturesque in flower planting, either for a flower garden or for flowers in borders. . . .*

It had to be admitted that the shape of the small suburban garden was all against it. 'It is obvious', Loudon says, 'that gardens thus shaped afford little opportunity for taste being displayed in laying them out.' So their chief interest must depend on their flora, and on their being kept constantly in a good state of cultivation and perfect tidiness.

Very little was to be done with the very tiny front garden. No large tree can be admitted there, for it will shade the windows of the house. You might have a flowerbed; probably the best thing was to have a few flowering shrubs intermingled with evergreens. If the front garden is usually in shade, plant arbutus, laurustinus and variegated hollies. Loudon does not here mention the plant which became the commonest inhabitant of hundreds of thousands of suburban front gardens later in the century: *Aucuba.* Yet he uses it elsewhere; perhaps he foresaw its dismal effect in miles of small and dusty and even sooty front gardens.

But in the back garden there is much more scope: but let the householder first consider what he wants: economy in planting and maintenance; profit in the form of produce; or ornament and enjoyment? If it be economy, then the garden should consist of a lawn with a few shrubs and trees. On the subject of the profitable suburban garden, the Loudons are discouraging; for, '... the vegetables grown in it generally cost more than they could be bought for from a greengrocer'. This, however, does not mean that one should not grow them, for some of them are so much better gathered fresh. So the suburban kitchen gardener should grow peas, cabbages and other greens, and also some culinary herbs. However, such a garden requires a great deal of care and attention to keep it in even tolerable order, and will look very untidy if neglected.

On the other hand, purely ornamental gardening is the most expensive:

In the neighbourhood of London the best way is to contract with a nurseryman to keep the garden in order, and full of flowers, at a given price per year; but as this takes away a great deal of the pleasure of the proprietor and his family in the garden (as we all like things of our own creation, better than what is done for us), a more agreeable plan is to have a gardener once a week to keep the place in order; and to fill the beds with greenhouse plants purchased from the people who hawk them about the streets. If the soil and situation are tolerably good, these plants will grow luxuriously, and produce abundance of flowers from May till September or October, when the plants will be killed by frost.

The Loudons then go on to give a variety of layouts under the three headings. It is obvious from those layouts for the most economical gardens, in which only lawns and shrubs are used, that Loudon had learnt a lot from his study of Humphry Repton.[65] Even in a small area, Loudon achieves a certain freedom, a pleasing look of nature. But the range of species recommended is very much wider than Repton used or would perhaps have approved; it includes almond and Judas trees, daphne, hypericum, philadelphus, crabs and mountain ashes, the pink-flowered pseudo-acacias (*Robinia*), brooms, sophoras, and even double-flowered gorse. Among the flowers recommended there are more annuals than we should use nowadays. The list of climbers for walls includes what must then have been some interesting novelties, *Clematis florida*, for example, *Bignonias* and the Banksian rose. One of the alternative plans is for a rose and fruit-tree garden without any perennial flowers.

Plans for kitchen gardens are illustrated and explained and their proper maintenance expounded with care and thoroughness. Fruit varieties are listed, with the particular qualities of each kind of fruit for cooking or table.

From these designs, layouts, planting plans and maintenance instructions for diverse kinds of very small gardens, the Loudons then go on to gardens of a quarter of an acre and upwards. For these Loudon seems to have worked out rules from Repton's theory and practice, modified for the smaller

scale. A measure of regularity is imposed by two conditions: the fact that suburban gardens are rectangular and fenced; and his own ideas for what he called 'gardenesque'. Yet within small areas Loudon did contrive 'natural' miniature landscapes, even vistas. Here the range of woody plants which he used is large—eighty species of small trees and evergreen shrubs and twenty-nine species of deciduous shrubs. On the plans the place for every plant is shown by keying. Loudon even gives prices for the plants, and a few examples may be of interest: all kinds of hawthorn cost 9*d* each; on the other hand, you had to pay 3*s*6*d* for a 'Yulan' magnolia. Tulip tree saplings were 6*d* each, but laburnums 1*s*6*d*, which seems odd. Hardy rhododendrons cost 6*d*, Liquidambars 1*s*, and variegated box were 6*d* each. A list of herbaceous perennials is given, but choice from it is left to 'the lady of the house', who is warned that as the trees and shrubs grow bigger, the perennials will not grow so well; and this also applies to rose bushes. The estimated cost of laying out a quarter-acre garden to a typical Loudon design, was as follows:

	£	s	d
The preparation of the ground *including the draining and the formation of the walks, in this garden; will cost about*	10	0	0
The trees required amount to about 67; *which at the above prices average 1s2d each (cash) and come to*	3	18	1
Shrubs and roses, 108	4	2	6
Climbing shrubs, 26		19	3
Herbaceous plants, annuals and biennials, 546; *and supposing the greater part of them to be annuals they may be purchased for*	6	6	0
In all	£25	5s	10d

Loudon estimates the annual maintenance cost at between £3 and £5.

The greater part of the Loudons' book was given up to much larger suburban gardens and does not concern us here. Its influence on the swiftly increasing number of what I call urban cottage gardens, that is the small suburban garden, was excellent. What was the influence of the Loudons with this book and with *The Manual of Cottage Gardening and Husbandry* (1830) on country cottage gardening? No doubt,

Preceding pages
GORDON PLACE, KENSINGTON, LONDON The cottage element is obvious in the way every small front garden in these terraces is crammed with flowers.

HIGHGATE, LONDON The sophisticated town gardener followed the cottager's example by mingling flowers and vegetables in a small space.

English Cottage Gardens

as I have said, it had an effect on the relatively small number of middle-class occupants of country cottages; but on the great majority, it was negligible, if only because the country cottager was too poor to benefit even from such carefully considered and soundly economical advice as Loudon's. One could not do much in the way of ornamental gardening on a weekly wage of 8s. So at this point we have two different classes of cottage garden to consider: the real country cottager's garden, still primarily a kitchen garden; and the ornamental cottage garden of the small number of middle-class cottagers in the country, whose gardens derive more from such planned small suburban gardens as Loudon devised than from the poor neighbour's country gardens. Whence, if not out of thin air and dreams, comes the cottage

Rural and Suburban

garden of romantic fiction, then? The answer is from the eighteenth-century survivals, like Old Sally's in Flora Thompson's remembrances and from cottage gardens imitated and improved from such models by garden-loving educated people, of small means, like, for example, Miss Mitford of *Our Village* fame. The ornamental quality of the farm-worker's or the rural craftsman's garden was accidental; the middle-class cottager now began to deduce rules from that accident and to interpret them in the light of writings like Loudon's, or of their own taste. And what emerged was the 'cottage garden' we all think of when the words are mentioned, that is, a particular kind of rustic prettiness, and not the garden made and cultivated for any purpose but ornament.

Front gardens at CRACOE, YORKSHIRE (*left*) and at KENSINGTON, LONDON (*right*) exhibit the profusion of a cottage-derived style.

Rural and Suburban

I shall continue to draw upon Flora Thompson in order to give some idea of the real cottager's garden in the later half of the nineteenth century, for I can think of no better guide. But there is this to be said, that in some parts of the country there were considerable differences; cottagers might be better off in the neighbourhood of a great house and estate, and their gardens less purely utilitarian; in the north there were special cases, like the Lancashire Gooseberry-club gardeners, or the flower-growing specialists among the weavers with their auricula clubs and ranunculas clubs. But by and large, her picture of the cottage garden is true for the greater part of the country.

The ordinary cottage had three rooms, no water laid on, and outdoor 'sanitation'. Everyone had a garden, and a great many also had allotments in place of the common rights which had been lost. The most important crop was probably potatoes, but,

The men took great pride in their gardens and allotments and there was always competition among them as to who should have the earliest and choicest of each kind. Fat green peas, broad beans as big as a halfpenny, cauliflowers a child could make an armchair of, runner beans and cabbages and kale. … Lettuce, radishes and onions.

Rosemary was grown for flavouring home-made lard used as a spread on bread. And that brings us to another import-ant cottage-garden produce: every cottage had a lean-to pigsty and a pig to fatten; the pig had a secondary role as a manure producer:

… the house refuse was thrown on a nearby pile called 'the muck'll'. This was situated so that the oozings from the sty could drain into it; the manure was also thrown there when the sty was cleared; and the whole formed a nasty, smelly eyesore to have within a few feet of the windows.

The vegetables were grown in the actual cottage plot; the allotments were given over half to the potatoes, half to wheat or barley. In the north the cereal crop might have been oats. The cottagers worked in their gardens and allot-ments even after a long, hard day on the farm, often hoeing by moonlight. Keeping a fine, clean tilth – 'touching 'er up a bit' – was considered the most important part of good gardening. In their gardens the men mostly had a few currant and gooseberry bushes, although the gooseberry never became as important in south and Midlands cottage gardens as in the north. And they also had 'a few old-fashioned flowers'.

Though the deliberate disorder of the London garden on the left derives from cottage garden example, the shaped bay tree, the vine and the irregular paving are in sharp contrast to the utilitarian concrete path and 'old fashioned' flowers of the garden at CHIPPING CAMPDEN, GLOUCESTERSHIRE (*right*).

English Cottage Gardens

The cottager's chief pride was in his potatoes, those potatoes which he had for so many centuries refused to admit to his garden at all. They grew several kinds, but the favourite was a variety called White Elephant:

Everybody knew that the elephant was an unsatisfactory potato, that it was awkward to handle when paring, and that it boiled down to a white pulp in cooking; but it produced tubers of such astonishing size that none of the men could resist the temptation to plant it.

A few of the gardens had raspberry canes and an apple tree. Soft fruit from both gardens and the hedgerows was made into jam. The women never worked in the vegetable gardens or the allotments, that was men's work, and even those whose children were off their hands did not touch it. But it was all right for them to grow flowers. Most cottages had a narrow border for flowers beside the path to the gate, and this was the woman's responsibility. There was no money for buying seeds, and the cottagers relied on gifts of cuttings and roots, or they kept seed from their own plants. The flowers grown were pinks and sweet williams, love-in-the-mist, wall-flowers, hollyhocks and michaelmas daisies. Most gardens had also lavender, rosemary, sweet briar and southernwood.

Almost every garden had its rosebush; but there were no coloured roses among them ... people had to be content with that meek, old-fashioned white rose with a pink flush at the heart, known as maiden's blush.

That, of course, would not have been the case everywhere; in other places, some other rose would have been the one grown in all the cottages; and elsewhere, in the more prosperous parts of the country, the cottagers might have had as many roses as Old Sally. Cottagers' wives also still cultivated a small bed or a few pots of herbs: thyme, parsley, sage, peppermint, pennyroyal, horehound, camomile, tansy, balm and rue were common, and all were in use, camomile as a general tonic, horehound in honey for sore throats and colds, peppermint tea as a ceremonial drink. Pennyroyal was used as an abortant, but Flora Thompson says that judging from appearances it was not very effective.

It is clear from the foregoing that there was a very great difference between the old country cottage gardens, still serving their ancient purpose, and the new suburban small gardens which were purely ornamental.

[8]
The Garden Press and the Horticultural Societies

Today's cottage gardener has available to him an enormous, indeed overwhelming, volume of printed guidance, and in addition he has radio and television programmes about every aspect of gardening. As he also has at his disposal, if he can afford it (which he sometimes can), light machine tools, a range of pest-control chemicals, and artificial fertilizers, one might suppose that if he is not completely and consistently successful in his gardening it must be his own fault. He need not even buy one of the popular gardening magazines if he does not want to, or listen to the radio programmes, or look at the television programmes, or buy, or borrow free from the public library (at the expense of the hard-working author) any of the thousands of books on every conceivable gardening subject which are there for the asking: he can simply read the gardening column in his daily or Sunday paper. Never, in the history of any craft, has a class of people been so pampered and coddled with cheap or free instructions; not that this argues any notable benevolence in our society: it is simply that the cottage garden is now big business because at long last the cottager has money to spend.

In 1969 there were twelve periodicals or part publications being published for the amateur gardener; five for the garden equipment trades; twenty-nine for the horticultural trade. In addition there were and are such monthly papers as *Homes and Gardens*, and the journals of the learned or specialist horticultural societies. Two hundred years ago there was no gardening paper of any kind.

The story of the growth of the gardening press has this in common with the progress of gardening in general: it began at a high social level and, as it were, worked its way downwards as literacy spread downwards through the social strata.

The first regular periodical publication of interest to gardeners was started in 1787: this was the *Botanical Magazine or Flower Garden Displayed*. It is more familiarly known as 'Curtis's Botanical Magazine' after its first editor and animating spirit, William Curtis. It published figures of flowering plants, hand-coloured; and described them. Curtis was an apothecary by trade, and he became a demonstrator in the Chelsea Physic Garden, which was, of course, a teaching garden. He discovered a remarkably fine botanical artist in a young Welshman named Sydenham Teast Edwards, and with his help and the backing of that great botanist and gardener the Earl of Bute, and a Quaker doctor, J.S.Lettsom – rich Quakers were very forward in the 'high gardening' of the time – Curtis made a remarkable success of his magazine, which is still published, although now by the Royal Horticultural Society and with the disadvantage that the plates have to be printed instead of hand-coloured.[66]

Next, in 1797, came *The Botanist's Repository*, and in 1815 *The Botanical Register* – both devoted, as indeed was Curtis's magazine, to figures and descriptions of rare exotics grown in British conservatories. All three magazines could really interest only the richer gardeners, and they were certainly of no use to cottagers, even to those who specialized so successfully in the cultivation of what were called 'Florists'' flowers (see below).

But in 1826 the already venerable publishing house of Longmans began publication of the *Gardeners' Magazine*, with J.C.Loudon, who was probably the promoter of the scheme, as managing editor; Loudon declared his purpose to be,

'. . . *to disseminate new and improved information on all topics connected with horticulture, and to raise the intellect and character of those engaged in this art*'.

This was a magazine for professional gardeners, and it dealt not only in technical horticultural matters, but in such social subjects as gardeners' wages and working conditions, which Loudon wanted to improve, and in the encouragement of horticultural societies, whose activities it was the first magazine to report. Loudon encouraged ordinary gardeners to write for the paper, even instructing them in how to do it:

. . . fix on a subject and begin it at once and write straight on to the end, regardless of anything but the correctness of your statements. This done once or twice, a good style will come of itself.[67]

Since most of the readers of the *Gardeners' Magazine* were working gardeners, it is likely that through them the magazine's teaching was passed on to hundreds of cottage gardeners, and sometimes, no doubt, the magazine itself. Be that as it may, it is certain that the *Gardeners' Magazine*

was the first horticultural periodical to be of use, if only at
second hand, to the cottager.

It had the field to itself for some years, during which time
it made Loudon £750 a year. But in 1841, Joseph Paxton,
the greatest gardener of the age (as some think; others would
prefer Loudon), who had started to learn his trade in his
father's cottage garden, who re-created Chatsworth, who
designed the great glass building which housed the Great
Exhibition–the Crystal Palace–who became a magnate, a
knight and a Member of Parliament, and who, when he
realized that he had had done all that he could in life, ended
it with a kind of Roman stoicism, started publishing what
was to become the most important magazine in the history
of the horticultural press: the *Gardeners' Chronicle*. Its backer
and publisher was Bradley of *Punch*, its botanical editor that
very distinguished botanist Professor Lindley, and its general
editor and driving force Joseph Paxton himself. The new
paper was registered as 'a stamped newspaper of rural
economy and general news', and its declared primary purpose was to be a 'weekly record of everything that bears upon
horticulture and garden botany'. Because Paxton's paper
carried general news as well as horticultural news and
features; because it carried the advertisements of nurserymen, garden sundries manufacturers, and situations vacant
and wanted, it soon became by far the most influential of the
gardening papers, written by and for professionals, but read
by amateurs as well. As a magazine for professionals, em-
ployers often paid the subscription so that their gardeners
could read it. From the first it was passed from hand to
hand, and it had, in this way, some circulation among cottage gardeners who could hardly have afforded to buy it.

But despite the success and growing sale of the *Gardeners'
Chronicle*, or maybe because of it, there seemed to to be
room for a gardening weekly addressed directly to cottagers
and small suburban gardeners. I say 'because of' that
success, for the obvious reason that Paxton's weekly had
created, among a larger and 'lower' class than ever before,
the habit of reading a gardening journal and relying on it
for instruction in gardening. At all events, the *Cottage
Garden* was started by G.W.Johnson in 1848. Johnson was
a barrister, but presumably a briefless one, for he not only
edited and published this magazine, but he wrote a history
of the English garden, the first thing of its kind, and edited
a *Cottage Gardeners' Dictionary* which, in later editions, became
simply the *Gardeners' Dictionary*.

English Cottage Gardens

This dropping of the word 'Cottage' must have been inspired by the growing importance of the suburban subscribers, who preferred to think of themselves as living in 'villas'. And in the same spirit, the *Cottage Gardener* continued as such until 1860, when the name was changed to *The Horticultural Journal* without any great change in the matter and manner of the paper. It was an admirable little production, somewhat pompous in its language and moralizing in tone, but showing a genuine concern for the improvement of the cottagers' gardens, although it catered also for a rather higher social class. The implication of the editor's introduction of his new paper in the first number is that there was, at that time, no horticultural magazine dealing with outdoor gardening. This was not true, although other papers did give a great deal of their space to conservatory work and tender exotic plants. Perhaps the *Gardeners' Chronicle* was regarded as being strictly a trade paper, not for the amateur.

Standing features in the *Cottage Gardener* must be some guide to the small gardener's interests in the mid nineteenth century: one is on garden pests; another on fruit growing; a third on the flower garden. A separate feature was devoted weekly to 'Florists' Flowers', cultivars of certain genera including tulips, ranunculas and auriculas; I shall have more to say about this aspect of cottage gardening in the nineteenth century in a moment. Another standing feature was devoted to the kitchen garden week by week, detailing the work to be done in it.

Johnson had a (valuable) bee in his bonnet about the use of house sewage as manure; he had constructed an ingenious contraption which filtered all the 'sewage' from his own house, and fed the resultant fluid, which he described as 'inoffensive' after filtration, by way of a system of gas pipes to his kitchen garden. The results in improved growth were spectacular, especially for his asparagus beds; the asparagus grew magnificently; and if the house sewage carried the cholera bacillus into the vegetable garden, Johnson's household survived, at least as far as I know. He published plans and drawings of his filtration devices, and urged that cottagers, especially poor cottagers, should adopt it for their own gardens, although admitting that it would only work if there was a steep fall in level from the house to the garden. Johnson returns to this theme again and again; and from the conservationist point of view he was certainly quite right.

He published excellent articles especially for the cottage gardener and allotment holder. The optimum crop figures

LONDON backyard. With nowhere else to garden, the English will garden in pots.

which he set for an eighth of an acre seem very high; the most important crop is the potato; a number of the articles between 1849 and 1860 deal with the rising incidence of potato blight, and there were contributions by readers on how to prevent or cure it, some of them flatly contradicting each other. Contributions from Ireland on this subject are treated as authoritative. An interesting experiment made by some Lancashire farmers received much attention: farmers with what was called 'mossland'–that is peat-bog soils– were getting them cleared and manured by letting them to cottagers, for potato growing, at 6*d* per perch; the farmer did the ploughing, and he carted the manure provided by the cottager. The cottager planted and cared for the crop, which was all his own; after one season of growing potatoes like this, the land would produce a good crop of corn.

A more or less regular feature in the paper briefly describes newly introduced plants, or newly selected cultivars– a crimson, double-flowered peach; *Zauscheneria californica* as a change from fuchias for the window-sill garden; a cucumber called, of all names, 'Prizefighter'; and then there is a very good new strawberry raised from Keen's Seedling.

A digression on the subject of this favourite fruit: strawberries, even the cottager's strawberries, had quite recently ceased to be the little native ones introduced from the wild and which, with careful cultivation, might produce fruit as large as a blackberry. *Fragraria virginiana* and *F. chiloensis* having been introduced in the eighteenth century from North and South America respectively, the French botanist Duchesne tried to cross them, failed, and then succeeded, accidentally, when he was not actually trying, in getting a chance seedling in a field where both species were cultivated. The resultant seedling and its vegetative offspring produced much larger fruit than the European native strawberries, the size being derived from the relatively large fruited Chilean native strawberry. French work on strawberries having been held up by the outbreak of the Revolution, it was taken up in England. Michael Keens made the same crosses as Duchesne, and he may also have had some of the new French plants; his success in obtaining a number of large-fruited seedling strawberries was later decried as mere luck by some professional breeders; the fact remains that he did produce strawberries larger and more succulent than any hitherto known, his best cultivar being Keen's Seedling, put into commerce in 1821. So completely English was this achievement of raising large-fruited strawberries that they were long known in France as *fraises anglaises*. Twenty years later, T.A.Knight, a founder member of the (later Royal) Horticultural Society, and a great breeder of fine fruits, was producing even better strawberries; perhaps the new one recommended by Johnson in his magazine was one of them.[68]

A personal experience, touching the matter of the cottage garden as a plant museum. During the 1950s I was engaged in reintroducing *remontant* autumn-fruiting strawberries into England, an article in *Country Life* having revealed that English gardeners did not even know that they existed.[69] At one time I had 140 varieties in cultivation from all over Europe and America.

These large-fruited autumn strawberries were originally bred in France; in a book I wrote on strawberry cultivation (*Strawberry Growing Complete*) I wrote:

The story is as follows: the parish priest of Chenoves (Seine-et-Loire) had long been experimenting with both Alpine strawberries and the fraises anglaises. *He produced a variety with a prolonged flowering and fruiting season, extending into the autumn, and large fruit. He claimed to have done this by crossing an Alpine strawberry variety with a* fraises anglaises *variety. Although no one else had, in fact, succeeded in doing this, there was at that time no scientific reason to doubt the claim of this enterprising ecclesiastic. It is only now, when we understand more of genetics, that we are forced to regard the Abbé Thivolet's claim with suspicion. All the Alpine varieties, being improved* F. vesca, *are diploid plants. The* fraises anglaises, *that is the large-fruited, short-seasoned midsummer strawberries, are all octoploids. Geneticists say that cross-fertilization between these is not possible, or rather that the resultant seed is sterile. There is no need to go into the reason for this: it derives from the fact that such a cross produces an uneven number of chromosomes in the gene, and that you cannot exactly halve an uneven number in units. It is not necessary to call the reverend gardener's good faith in question. He no doubt went through the motions of fertilizing a flower of some Alpine variety with the pollen of some large-fruited variety. One of the seedlings became the prototype of the perpetuals. Probably a fortuitous mutation was the real origin of the new variety: some of the ordinary varieties have a tendency to crop a second time in the autumn.*

It seemed to me unlikely that these excellent fruits had never been introduced into Britain. I discovered that they had and that they had gone out of favour. I then began trying to locate survivors; and at last I found a few plants of what

were almost certainly the Abbé Thivolet's 'Saint Joseph' in two cottage gardens, one in Lancashire and one in County Wicklow in Ireland.

One of the several origins of village horticultural societies chiefly composed of cottage gardeners, and which we shall come to presently, can, I think, be found in the annual dinners, with prizes for champion crops, sometimes given by benevolent landlords to allotment tenants, as reported in the *Cottage Gardener*. The landlord paid for the dinner, there might be as many as fifty guests; and he gave money prizes for the best vegetable or fruit in a number of 'classes'.

Educational articles in the magazine were good: the reader was taught how to take geranium cuttings, how to look after window-sill gardens made on the Loudon model, how to improve poor soils; how to make best use of night-soil as manure; how to cultivate new plants, even such exotics as the New Zealand *Clematis indivisa*. The recognition of garden pests feature, with enlarged drawings of the insect pests clearly engraved, continued for many years. An article on the raising of dwarf, precociously fruiting apple trees from cuttings is of particular interest in view of the work on this which is only now being done by Wye College.

There can be no question that the *Cottage Gardener* was the best help which had, until the mid nineteenth century, been offered to a class of gardeners who had, until then, had to manage with word-of-mouth advice and traditional lore which was often unsound. But it does seem as if Johnson was driven to look for his readers in a slightly more fortunate class than that of the cottagers, too many of whom, with a wage of 10s a week or even less, could hardly afford his paper, although one copy might be used by a dozen or more of them. Hence the change of name to the *Horticultural Journal* in 1860; and a slight change in favour of more sophisticated gardening.

The next important gardening periodical to be started was called first *The Garden*, and then later *Gardening Illustrated*; this was started in 1879 by one of the greatest gardeners in the history of English gardening, William Robinson. But although Robinson was himself born into the poorest class and the garden of his childhood must have been a cottage one, this paper's circulation and success was among middle- and upper-class gardeners and it was never a cottager's paper. But in 1884 came *Amateur Gardening*, directed to the small gardener in both town and country; it was not an immediate success, but when, three years later, a former working gardener called Thomas W. Sanders was appointed

Preceding pages
FINCHINGFIELD,
ESSEX.
Hyacinths were among the 'Florists' Flowers' favoured by the cottage garden societies in the eighteenth and nineteenth centuries. Ornamentals have here replaced the fruit trees former cottagers grew on their walls.

editor the paper became very successful and won readers even from the *Gardeners' Chronicle*. It has remained the most popular gardening weekly among both country cottagers and urban gardeners and is now edited by Mr Anthony Huxley. Its contribution towards the further horticultural education of cottagers and suburbanites has been a very considerable one. Its present weekly sale is well over 200,000 copies; but its readership is very much larger than that: about a million and a half.[70] Of these it is estimated that about 400,000 are country cottagers. The other large circulation gardening weekly *Popular Gardening*, after merging with *Home Gardening* and *The Smallholder*, has a weekly sale of something under 200,000 and a cottage readership which must be something like a quarter of a million; however, this was not started until the 1930s. By then the cottage gardener was getting his horticultural news and views from another source.

The BBC broadcast the first gardening talk – 'Gardening at Easter' – in March 1923, the speaker being E.G.Evans; in the same year L.Cook broadcast a talk on *Rose Gardening round London*, and C.Harding on *Gardening in April*. Then, in April 1924, began a series of talks on gardening – the Royal Horticultural Society talks – which went on at regular intervals until October 1926. These were the days of the simple crystal receiving set, and hundreds of thousands of people made their own sets, so that the habit of listening spread rapidly. The first gardening series for the north was started in the Liverpool studios in 1927. The first popular gardening broadcaster, Marion Cran, originally broadcast in August 1923 and continued to do so throughout the Savoy Hill days of the BBC's early career – 'This is 2 LO calling' – and into the 1930s, acquiring a following of listeners numbered in millions.

The BBC's most famous gardening broadcaster, C.H. Middleton, broadcast his first talk of *The Week in the Garden* series in May 1931. Middleton was the son of a head gardener, but, tall and elegant, looked more like a professional man. He lived in a London suburb and the garden his talks were based on was a typical small suburban one, ninety paces long, surrounded by the other little gardens. *The Week in the Garden* ran for six years and was succeeded by Middleton's *In Your Garden* programme, which was his until he died in May 1945. He had, by then, an audience of millions and the largest radio fan mail in the country. During his summer holidays one of the speakers who stood in for him had been Fred Streeter, another cottager born, but by then head gardener at Petworth. Streeter took up the programme and became as successful and nationally famous a garden broadcaster as Middleton. The Chairmanship of this immensely successful programme was taken on by Mr Roy Hay, editor of the *Gardener's Chronicle*. *In Your Garden*, with various speakers and with Fred Streeter as the permanent star of the programme, ran for many years.

Roy Hay is the son of Tom Hay, who was formerly Superintendent of the Royal Parks and one of the most famous gardeners of his time. As well as becoming editor of *The Gardeners' Chronicle*, Mr Hay became Gardening Correspondent of *The Times*—he still is. He gave his first broadcast in 1936. In 1950 the BBC gave him a programme of his own—*Home Grown*—with Fred Streeter as adviser to listeners on the week's work in the garden, and with different speakers every week, including, on numerous occasions, myself.

Television's star of gardening programmes, Mr Percy Thrower, is another case of a celebrated garden specialist born to a cottage garden, as it were; he began work at fourteen as a gardener's boy, was a gardener at Windsor Castle when he was eighteen, and in due course became Shrewsbury's Parks Superintendent; he holds the National Diploma in Horticulture, the highest qualification in England. He first broadcast in 1946; his *Gardening Club* television programme started in January 1956 and ran for nearly twelve years.

Reverting to the pre-broadcasting era, how did all the flood of garden literature—and it should be remembered that even today each copy of the popular gardening periodicals is read by seven people and that in the past the number was even greater[70]—actually affect the cottage garden? By introducing the cottage gardener to new plants or varieties or cultivars of old ones, it enriched the cottage garden flora, chiefly in those parts of the country where the cottager was not as poor as those of Larkrise; and, of course, the hundreds of thousands of suburban gardens; it taught the small gardener rules, skills and tricks of the trade which he had not known before; it improved garden equipment, and garden order and hygiene. It did something even more important: for the first time it brought the cottager into the national company of men who were using brains, education, taste and imagination in the one art, a minor one if you like, but still an art, which every cottager could try to practise; in other words, the cottager was at long last admitted to share his country's 'culture', for at least one of its manifestations was put within his understanding. It is no wonder that nine million Englishmen and women are gardeners.

NORTHAM, SUSSEX
From the seventeenth century onwards tulips increased in popularity and variety. The tulip was one of the eight kinds of flowers designated 'Florists' Flowers' by the florist society of cottagers.

The third great influence which changed some of the ancient ways of cottage gardening was that of the clubs and societies of gardeners. I have suggested above that one of their several origins were the dinners given by some landlords to their allotment tenants, reported in the *Cottage Gardener*. But there were other and more direct origins; of more interest than allotment holders' dinners were the gooseberry shows and florists' societies of the north country.

An interesting difference between the movement to form such societies in the south, and that in the north, a difference which will come as no surprise to northcountrymen, is that whereas in the south the movement had to be started and for some time maintained by the gentry, or at least the clergy, in the north the movement came from the people themselves: industrial proletariats are always more independent and always have more social initiative than rural workers. Granted that one must always make an honourable exception for Joseph Archer and the Tolpuddle Martyrs, it is nevertheless true that south of England villagers remained dependent on leadership from above for very much longer than north of England cottager-operatives.

There will be a Gooseberry meeting held at the house of Mr John Leech, The Brown Cow, Glodwick Lane, near Oldham. The spring meeting to be on the first Saturday in January, the making-up the last Saturday in March, and the day of weighing the first Saturday in August. The same regulations to be adopted as are agreed by the Rochdale people. The landlord purposes giving four copper kettles and Francis Clegg will give an excellent garden spade to the person who wins the first prize. The second prize will be put out with a ribband of good quality. Any person residing above five miles off may become a member by sending 3s6d for his subscription to the spring meeting, and be exempt for 1s of ale.

This notice dated 1821, is typical of notices which went out all over the Lancashire, Cheshire and Staffordshire districts from at least as early as 1812 (the dates of the earliest gooseberry show schedule in the collection of the Royal Horticultural Society at the Lindley Library).[71] The shows were nearly always held at public houses and inns, and no doubt the landlords did all they could to encourage them, offering prizes, as John Leech does in the above notice. There were several classes, but as a rule only three, red, yellow and green gooseberries, and there was a prize or prizes in each class. The all time champion gooseberry seems to have been one weighing 28 dwt troy, nearly two ounces avoirdupois; but the top weights in most shows were of the order of 20½ dwt, equivalent to twelve gooseberries to the pound avoirdupois. About twenty varieties of gooseberries were grown, and two which seem to have often produced winners were 'Triumphant' and 'Crown Bob'.

That the men who took part in the gooseberry shows, using all kinds of their own devices, such as 'feeding' individual fruits on solutions of sugar, to increase the size of their show fruit, did not confine themselves to growing gooseberries is obvious from the fact that some of the schedules contain a page or two of flower-show schedule, the 'classes' being, as a rule, for 'florists' flowers (see below).

In the northern industrial counties, then, the gooseberry shows were ancestral to the more general small horticultural societies.

In other parts of the north country, including Yorkshire and Derbyshire, and above all in the lowland counties of Scotland, horticultural societies had their origin in the earlier florists' societies whose members were mill operatives. There seems to me to be something very moving in the way these people, who lived the best part of their lives in and surrounded by the 'dark satanic mills', turned for relief to the exquisitely careful growing of the most delicate hardy flowers, and competed with their skill and knowledge to produce ever more perfect strains.

Eight kinds of plants were designated 'florists' flowers by the rules of these florists' societies: tulip, auricula, carnation, pink, ranunculas, hyacinth, anemone and polyanthus. These were the favourites of the seventeenth- and early-eighteenth-century gentry; and here we have a clear case of the cottage gardener preserving and even further improving garden flowers which had more or less ceased to be fashionable in the great gardens (one must except the tulip perhaps), although some of them were to be restored to fashion in due course.

The auricula is to be found in the highest perfection in the gardens of the manufacturing class who bestow much time and attention on this and a few other flowers, as the tulip and the pink. A fine stage of these plants is scarcely ever to be seen in the gardens of the nobility and gentry, who depend upon the exertions of hired servants, and cannot therefore compete in these nicer operations of gardening with those who tend their flowers themselves, and watch over their progress with paternal solicitude.[72]

Although the tulip is mentioned in the above-quoted passage, in practice the north country 'manufacturing' cottagers tended to leave that to richer amateurs; they could not afford the really rare tulip bulbs, which towards the end of the eighteenth century sometimes cost as much as £50 apiece, more than a year's wages. A famous tulip grower who had a nursery at Gibs Heath near Soho is said to have spent £3,000 on rare bulbs during thirty-five years of growing them; and as late as the 1830s that grower's son still had tulip bulbs at prices up to £20 each for sale.[73] That kind of thing was clearly not for the industrial cottager.

Loudon, in his *Encyclopaedia of Gardening*, records William Ferrier of Paisley as writing that the extraordinary skill of his parishioners in the breeding of the exquisite new pinks for which they had become famous was in a measure due to the delicacy of their daily work in the weaving of very fine patterned muslins, and the devising of new and ever more finely wrought patterns. The Paisley weavers had raised a number of seedlings with the kind of marking called 'lacing' from a consignment of seed procured in London; they bought more seed from the same source, found a few more laced pinks among the seedlings, and began, by crossing, selection and segregation, to produce more and more perfect specimens of variations on these original patterns. One sees the strength of Mr Ferrier's comparison. These laced pinks were soon in great demand by pink specialists all over England, as well as Scotland.

The carnation 'florists' had to produce flowers, for show, to an astonishing standard of perfection: Loudon says that the stems had to be stout and straight and between thirty and forty-five inches long; the flowers, which must be three inches in diameter to qualify, were as nearly as possible perfect hemispheres, full but not crowded with petals, the imbrication to be even and regular, the colours distinct and in regular stripes on a pure white ground, excepting in the case of the Picotee class, which had spotted markings and whose petals had to have a serrated margin.[74]

Florists' hyacinths and anemones were of comparatively few kinds. But there were more than 800 kinds of florists' ranunculas, with an astonishing range of colours from pale primrose through all the yellows to orange; from pale pink through all the pinks and reds to deep crimson; and from olive through a range of browns to black – this would probably have been a very deep purple, 'black' in certain lights. All these ranunculas belonged to the same species, *Ranuncula asiaticus*, including the straked, brindled and mottled classes.

Yet other florists' societies specialized in the two kinds of primula recognized as 'florists' flowers, the auriculas referred

The cottage window-sill at BAWDSEY, SUFFOLK (*top*), is a crowded miniature garden, vying with the plot outside, while at BRADWELL-JUXTA-MARE, ESSEX (*below*) a cottager with no front garden resorts, in emulation of the townsman, to the window-box and hanging basket. The stones of the path at WELCOMBE, NORTH DEVON (*below right*) like the roof slates of the porch are of local origin and provide the right setting for the arabis so often found in West Country cottage gardens.

The Garden Press and the Horticultural Societies

to as being brought to perfection only in the operatives' cottage gardens; and polyanthus. Polyanthus had to be bright scarlet, or deep crimson, or chocolate-brown, the 'eye' sulphur or lemon-yellow, matching the lacing of the margins. Not only were the finest strains of laced polyanthus bred in cottage gardens in the north, but they were preserved in cottage gardens all over the country, yet had become quite rare when, a couple of decades ago, a taste for them was revived among sophisticated middle-class gardeners.

As for the auricula, it had, of course, been a collector's favourite in the seventeenth century, like the tulip, and men like Evelyn, Rea and Hanmer devoted much care to it and swopped plants with each other or made each other presents of rare plants. But by the nineteenth century it was hardly to be found among such people, and the finest strains, with flowers whose colours were incomparably subtle and included greys and blue-greens, were all in cottage gardens, for the most part in Lancashire, Cheshire and parts of lowland Scotland. Not that all the auricula specialists were mill operatives; the most famous of them, George Lightbody, was a former naval warrant officer, a hero twice captured by the Americans in the American War of 1812. He settled down as a professional 'florist' after leaving the navy, doubtless with some prize money to invest; started on auriculas with three expensive champion plants, paying as much as £3 15s for a single one, and raised thousands of seedlings, the best of which made him famous among gardeners everywhere.[75] Still, for the most part the great auricula growers were certainly north country cottagers, and from their shows and societies developed the more general horticultural societies of the second half of the century.

A very great stimulus to the formation of horticultural societies was the growing fame of *the* Horticultural Society, (not yet 'Royal'), in London.

This had first been mooted by John Wedgwood, son of the great potter, Josiah Wedgwood, in 1801. Wedgwood started the ball rolling by writing about his plan to found a Horticultural Society to William Forsyth, George III's gardener at Kensington. At Wedgwood's suggestion Forsyth showed the plan to the grand panjandrum of all the sciences, the great botanist and real begetter of Kew Gardens as we know them, Sir Joseph Banks. Wedgwood was a banker by profession, an artist by inclination – he had studied painting under Flaxman – and an enthusiastic and clever gardener. When Banks approved his plan, other amateurs and profes-

Ornaments such as the plant-filled wheelbarrow and the stone ball at AIRTON, YORKSHIRE, only found their way into cottage gardens when the cottagers had become middle class.

sionals were brought in, including the dilettante but brilliant collector of rare plants, precious stones and beautiful mistresses, Charles Greville, second son of the Earl of Warwick; and William Townsend Aiton, who had followed his father as curator of Kew Gardens.

It is not my business here to say much about the astonishing career of what was and remains by far the greatest horticultural society in the world, with some 80,000 Fellows. By becoming a national institution, although only after many vicissitudes, it was able to raise the standard of gardening throughout England to new heights of excellence. And its very existence created that 'climate' in the world of horticulture which was most favourable to the formation of local horticultural societies. By 1825, according to the *Gardener's Magazine*'s accounts of the transactions and activities of such societies, there were 196 of them in England and Scotland. There were probably many more with which the magazine did not happen to have correspondents. If cottage membership was at first small, it grew rapidly larger. These societies held one or two annual shows, and by competitions raised the standard of gardening in all its branches. In due course, the hundreds, at last thousands, of such societies accepted the rules of the Royal Horticultural Society for the judging of their competitions, and also for the definition of the many classes of vegetables, fruit and flowers.

So, then, the Loudons, the horticultural press, and the horticultural societies brought the cottager gardener into the modern age of gardening. But it did not much change the shape and layout of the cottage garden; for the most part, the cottager continued to plant flowers and vegetables together in rows, although he now might, like the Larkrise gardeners, have a bed devoted only to flowers. There was an improvement in the quality of garden varieties of all kinds of plants, and in their cultivation.

[9]
Cottagers' Roses

It has, I hope, been made clear that, sentimental notions about the cottage garden notwithstanding, there is not and never has been any real distinction between garden flowers in general and cottage garden flowers. It is true that by the nineteenth century the eight florists' flowers mentioned in Chapter Eight were to be found commonly in cottages, although more commonly in industrial operatives' cottages than in gentlemen's gardens; perhaps it was that which gave rise to the idea of certain flowers as being specifically cottagey; but as we have seen these flowers were simply kinds which had formerly been favourites in the greater gardens of the gentry, and had fallen victims to fashion for other kinds of ornamental plants. I repeat that the apparent distinction was owed to the cottager's poverty which, by preventing him from buying the latest garden plants, kept his garden 'backward'; this 'backwardness' was then given a pleasanter name and image by English sentimentality about old-fashioned things and the 'good old days'. Thus the particular kind of sweetness and prettiness of the simple cottage garden became an object of admiration.

There is, however, something else to be added: the fact is that those who admired, and in the end started to imitate, a kind of garden and gardening which were the fortuitous products of certain economic and social conditions were, in a measure, aesthetically right. By accident the cottage garden accomplished something worth doing. Progress in the breeding and selection of specifically garden plants has entailed the loss of the qualities of the original species, the plant breeder's raw material: grace, simple perfection of form, and often fragrance vanished to be replaced by greater size, more and richer colours and other attributes considered desirable by sophisticated gardeners. And the loss of the original qualities of the species was progressive. If anyone doubts this, let him think of the monstrous and hideous garden calceolarias and compare them with the species; of some of the huge and blowsy garden begonias; of the blown-up delphiniums when compared with the species delphiniums; of the huge 'Dutch' crocuses side by side with the species from which they were developed; of the enormous and gaudy garden gladiolus compared with the botanical species; of the modern roses, such as 'Peace', by comparison with the older hybrids or with the wild roses. If there is, from one point of view – that of bulk and flamboyance – a gain, the losses are obvious and grievous. One cannot call the big garden flowers 'unnatural'; it is simply that the attributes potential in a genus cannot be fully realized until its species, separated in nature by distances which make intercrossing, and therefore full exploitation of the genes, impossible, are brought together in one place by the plant collector and the gardener so that the whole gene pool of that genus comes into play. A genus in which both gains and losses are most apparent is *Rhododendron*: one cannot but admire the skill with which, out of the species, breeders have created hardy shrubs whose floriferousness, colours and vigour are overwhelming; but look, then, at some of the species, especially the Chinese species, and see what has been lost.

But since the cottage gardener's poverty kept him one, two or many steps behind in the race to supplant species with garden varieties, old cultivars with new ones, the loss, in the cottage garden, was much slower, and a measure of the simpler grace of the wild flower was usually to be found in the cottage garden when it had vanished elsewhere. From time to time a gardener of taste from one of the higher social levels, perhaps a gardening trend-setter like Gertrude Jekyll or Victoria Sackville-West, would realize what had been sacrificed in the business of increasing the size and vigour, sturdiness and floriferousness of ornamental plants and, seeking to restore grace and simplicity, find the means to do so in some cottager's garden. Moreover, the sophisticated middle-class cottager, by imitating the real cottager's garden, turned an accident into a style, so that rules for that kind of gardening could be deduced.

The process has been, as I have said, progressive; and it can be rather roughly reconstructed in the case of the plant which long has been and still is by far the most important garden ornament: the rose.

The roses grown in the earliest English gardens to have any flowers at all, and *à plus forte raison*, in cottage gardens before the fifteenth century and for some time into that

From the mid-nineteenth century hybrid roses like these at CRANBROOK, KENT, began to dominate cottage gardens.

Cottager's Roses

century, were the native species transplanted from the wild, just like other woody plants such as honeysuckles, privets, raspberries, the ribes, and, of course, strawberries. These natives are *Rosa canina*, the common dog rose; *R. arvensis*, from which we had the earliest 'rambler' roses; the Burnet roses, *R. spinossissima*; and the 'Sweet Briar' *R. eglanteria*, valued for its fragrant foliage, used as a medicinal herb, and one of the earliest and pleasantest of hedge plants. It should not be supposed that, after a certain lapse of time, these wild roses in gardens remained identical with the average hedge-row or moorland roses. From time immemorial men have transplanted from the wild not just any specimen of the species they admired or had a use for, but the most remarkable specimens – those showing exceptional richness of colour, size of flower, doubling perhaps, or some other more or less spectacular attribute. So that from the beginning there has been a measure of selection; and the segregation in gardens of outstanding individuals of certain species, resulting in selfing or in crossing only between such remarkable individuals, has tended to accentuate and even to fix the superior attributes of such plants in garden varieties, that is in cultivars, which were then, for their good qualities, propagated vegetatively, and so perpetuated. So doubtless the wild roses of early English cottage gardens were superior to the wild rose of the wayside.

The second 'generation' of garden roses – I am not using the word in its literal and correct sense, but rather as engineers talk of a 'generation' of aeroplanes – was derived from a south European wild rose, *R. centifolia*. It is not now known in the wild and its habitat is not discoverable. It is no doubt the oldest rose in cultivation and was perhaps grown in the gardens of the ancient Near Eastern proto-civilizations. Among the derivatives of *R. centifolia* are the cabbage roses, the Provence roses, the moss roses, the Burgundy roses and the pompon roses. All these 'races' of roses were introduced into England in the course of the fifteenth century. Needless to say, they were not so introduced by cottagers, but by monks or their abbots, and by châtelains, and it must have been the case that, as rare and expensive novelties, they were for a long time confined to the courtyard and cloister gardens of castles, manor houses and monasteries. But all of these roses are very easily increased by cuttings and layers; slowly stocks became common; the native English roses were supplanted in the gardens of the great by these new garden roses. Meanwhile, they remained in the cottage gardens; and it may well be

HENDON, MIDDLESEX
Urban and suburban small gardeners were quicker than country cottage gardeners to reject old roses in favour of new.

[127]

that even in those days there were sophisticated ladies who, sick of the flamboyance of the new roses, praised the simple charm of the old ones, the cottager's eglantine or Burnet rose.

In the next century, the great men's gardens were enriched with introductions other than the centifolia derivatives. It is possible that *R. damascena*, since it is said to have been brought home by a crusader, may have been even earlier in gardens here than those. Then came *Rosa* 'Alba', an Italian hybrid between the Damascus and the dog rose; in due course, it became the white rose of York, so it was not later than the fifteenth century in England. The damask rose gave rise also to striped and straked roses, notably the 'York and Lancaster', which was still in Old Sally's Larkrise garden, though such striped bicolour roses in modern gardens are more usually the variety *versicolor* of *R. gallica*, a rose which reached us from south Europe before the end of the sixteenth century, as did also the sweetscented musk rose, *R. moschata*, and the Persian yellow rose, *R. foetida*. In due course, the very oldest garden varieties of roses, pushed out by novelties from the rich man's garden, supplanted the old wild roses in the cottage garden.

Not only did each 'generation' of newly introduced roses linger in the cottage garden after being turned out of the great garden, and so become the 'old-fashioned' roses of the time; there was another way in which cottage garden roses became perpetually old fashioned. The pedigree of any modern rose is so immensely complicated that it can no longer be traced in detail, but only in very broad lines: as more and more roses were introduced, first from Europe, then from the Near East, from Iran, China, India and America, accidental and deliberately made crosses produced increasingly numerous hybrids.

All these roses were more or less variable themselves, but the combination of their characters with those of other species has widened the range of varieties to an almost incredible extent.[76] From time to time a rose, or a group of roses, or a 'race' of roses would become the garden fashion; and older roses would be got rid of to make room for them; they would, perhaps, be passed on to a cottager who, propagating them by cuttings, would hand out plants to his friends and neighbours. So that the cottage gardens of parts of England became, as it were, museums for old hybrid rose cultivars, as well as for other 'old-fashioned' flowers.

At all events, the third generation of garden roses was largely composed of the variations, and chance hybrid seedlings, of the fifteenth- and sixteenth-century introductions.

Cottager's Roses

There seems then to have been a longish interval before any new 'blood' was introduced. This does not mean that there was no change in the rose population of England for a long time. The process I have described was not sudden, but continuous and relatively slow: this third 'generation' was only fully realized in all its variations and crossings after a very long period of time; in fact, it is a process which cannot, in the nature of living creatures, ever be finished. The original imported and native plant material might long remain the same without any new introductions; its derivatives became yearly more and more numerous and more diverse; the original introductions were, as it were, waves; but now there was a more or less steady flow, a never-ebbing tide, of novelties, fashion after fashion in roses; and always the cottage garden, receiving those plants which the manor garden no longer wanted, unintentionally but usefully preserved the beauties of the past.

The next important introduction of a new species was *R. sempervirens*, which reached us from France in 1629. This was a vigorous climber or trailer; and its genes ultimately gave to some garden roses an aptitude to give rise to climbing 'sports' of bush roses. So the roses-round-the-door cottage tradition is not older than the seventeenth century at the earliest, unless we suppose that some very early cottage porches were decorated with *R. arvensis*; actually, honeysuckles seem to have been chosen as decorative climbers, rather than roses. But once the climbing roses resulting from *R. sempervirens* had been replaced by more spectacular ones as the climbing habit was more widely acquired, then the oldest ones became, in the usual way, cottage roses, 'old-fashioned' roses, to be sought by those weary of the more sophisticated kinds and longing for the ancient simplicities: old plants are recovered from cottage gardens in much the same way as old furniture, banished to an attic by some change in fashion, is recovered by a new generation which again sees its merit.

As I have suggested, throughout the history of garden roses the movement from the manor garden, the gardens of great houses into cottage gardens, was a sort of slow and fairly steady drift. But from time to time there would be a sort of tidal wave, a new 'race' of garden roses would almost sweep the older ones out of the rich man's garden into the gardens of people who could not afford to buy novelties. Something like this followed the introduction, in 1768, of *R. chinensis*, which started to change the flowering habit of garden roses because of its gene for almost perpetual flowering: its derivatives were the monthly roses; and those miniatures known as 'fairy' roses (*R. lawranceana* and *R. roulettii*) which, after they had been almost lost to gardening, were recovered from a Swiss window-sill garden. During this and the immediately following periods of rose fashions, there were vogues for hybrid musks, hybrid perpetuals, and each in its turn was relegated to the cottage garden and there, for a while, preserved, often for long enough to be still there when the taste for it revived. We can best sum up the progress of the garden rose, from the 'wild' garden roses of the early fifteenth century to the mid nineteenth century by reference to the rose nurseryman's catalogue which John Claudius Loudon considered to be the best in his day: that of the nursery which was founded by John Rivers in 1725. In 1836 Rivers were offering:

Hybrid perpetuals (*derived from R. chinensis and some of the older garden races, thenursery recommending a June pruning to produce a good flush of flowers in autumn: 50 kinds.*
Hybrid China roses (*derived from R. chinensis and other races of older garden roses, and including Rivers's George IV said to be the finest hybrid rose yet raised): 89 kinds.*
Provence (cabbage) roses (*remarkable for their scent which was being lost in the newer roses): 25 kinds.*
Moss roses (*including the deep crimson novelty, Rouge du Luxembourg): 24 kinds.*
Rosa X 'Alba' cultivars (*I think that the old Maiden's Blush of the Larkrise gardens may have been one of these: they were white or pink): 25 kinds.*
Damasks: *19 kinds.*
Gallicas (' . . . *the spotted, striped and marbled roses in this section are very beautiful'): 90 kinds.*
Climbing roses: *53 kinds.*
R. indica derivatives (*misnomer, these roses were Chinese, not Indian): 70 kinds.*
Tea-scented China roses (*these resulted from the still recent introduction of R. odorata from China): 51 kinds.*
Fairy roses: *16 kinds.*
Noisette roses (*these derived from a China rose X musk rose cross made by John Champneys of Charleston USA*)[77]: *66 kinds.*
Bourbon roses (*newly introduced from France): 38 kinds.*
Musk roses: *10 kinds.*

Shrub roses harmonize with the flint and brick of these cottages at LAKENHEATH, SUFFOLK.

Cottager's Roses

R. bracteata (Macartney) derivatives: *10 kinds.*
Sweet briars: *17 kinds.*
Scotch roses (*R. spinossissima*): *27 kinds.*

There are a few more, not classified, such as the Banksian roses: in all more than 640 kinds of garden rose.

Which were the cottage roses of the 1840s and 1850s? Not the Bourbons, not the Noisettes, but the old damask and Provence roses. Yet by the end of the century you would probably have had to look for such 'old-fashioned' roses as George IV or Rouge du Luxembourg, by then nameless, in a cottage garden. There were, of course, roses which were never either fashionable or unfashionable, but merely useful, like the sweet briars and the Scotch roses. But when the hybrid musks came back into favour earlier in this century, it was in cottage gardens that they were found, before the German nurserymen began to repeat the old breeding programmes and produce new ones.

To millions of gardeners today, not only in England but all over the world, the word roses means hybrid tea and floribunda roses. And the old process is still continuing, despite the relative affluence of the cottage gardener in the second half of the twentieth century; middle-class people, buying an old house, and finding the floribundas of the equally middle-class but older vendor in the garden, dig them up and present them to the builders' workmen who are decorating the house. The builders' workmen could as well afford new roses as the man who gives him these old plants; but the habit of horticultural economy, of getting your plants free, dies hard.

The first hybrid tea rose was introduced into commerce in 1873. It was, like those which came after it, a cross between a hybrid perpetual and a tea-scented China rose. By that time some hybrid perpetuals, of which Rivers had listed about thirty kinds at the middle of the century, had probably made their way into cottage gardens near to great gardens, but they were still the fashionable roses, and indeed a lot of them were retained in big gardens well into the twentieth century. At first the colour range of the hybrid tea roses was restricted. Moreover, there was an element of tenderness to be overcome. One of the factors which helped to keep the early tea-scented roses confined to big gardens where there existed means of protecting difficult plants, was that *R. odorata*, from south-west China and rather tender, conveyed its tenderness to its offspring. It was first introduced in 1845,

Just as in cottage England an old rose climbing about the door might transform rural delapidation into picturesque charm, so the bleak lines and machine-made brick of this modern council house at THETFORD, NORFOLK, are softened and humanized by the new varieties of climbers rioting over the prosaic entrance.

but the French had been using it for breeding purposes before then; and the work of breeding tea-scented roses was largely left to them because, in the south, they had a suitable climate, which we did not. But beginning in 1853 there was a hardier 'race' of these new roses, the prototype being Gloire de Dijon.

By introducing other hybrid races of garden roses into the breeding programme, hybrid tea roses were given a much greater colour range and normal hardiness; inevitably a greater variation in the perfect form of the flowers was also introduced – centres which were higher or lower, more petals, or fewer – so that some hybrid teas actually reverted to being singles; and there were big differences in vigour, height and foliage. Fragrance, retained in the reds, or some of them, was entirely lost in many of the other colours; and the older hybrid perpetuals are still much better for scent. But the influence of fashion, the attraction of novelty, was, as usual, triumphant, and the hybrid teas were soon pushing the hybrid perpetuals out of the gardens of the sophisticated into the gardens of the poor.

Of all the 'races' or 'generations' of garden roses since the fifteenth century, none has had a shorter fashionable career than the polyantha roses. About the third quarter of the last century, someone had the idea of crossing one of the new hybrid teas – as this was not later than 1875, it must have been one of the first, for they were not generally distributed until 1890 at the earliest – with a Far Eastern species – it is widely distributed in nature over China, Japan and Korea – called *R. multiflora*, which bears its flowers in large panicles of numerous individuals. Its variety, *Platyphylla*, with rose-pink to crimson double flowers, was the Seven Sisters rose of old Sally's Larkrise garden. The result of the cross was twofold: a new race of 'polyantha' pillar roses; and the dwarf polyanthas, short and sturdy bush roses with single flowers in panicles. They seem never to have been very popular; but being crossed with other hybrid teas, they gave rise to the garden race of polyanthas roses. And if that race was short-lived in big gardens, and very soon banished in the usual way into cottage gardens, it was because it was quickly displaced by a superior garden race of roses bearing their flowers in panicles: the floribundas.

These are deserving of special mention in our context, because twentieth-century cottagers, at last in a position to buy their own garden plants instead of always waiting to be given them, have shown a marked preference for them over

Suburban influence has determined the sharp edges and rigid arrangement of this garden at STOCK PLAIN, YORKSHIRE, with its stiff rows of standard roses held firmly in place by staves much thicker than their stems. The layout of the garden perfectly accords with the emphatic, mechanical pointing of the masonry.

the hybrid teas; so have a lot of other gardeners, for they make a great show for very little trouble.

In the early 1920s the Danish rose-breeder Svend Poulsen crossed some single and some semi-double hybrid tea roses with some of the polyanthas. This gave rise to the so-called Poulsen roses, most of which have trusses of semi-double flowers. This kind of cross being repeated, but with fully double hybrid teas, the resultant garden race had trusses of miniature hybrid tea flowers in as great a range of colours as the latest hybrid teas. These were given the name 'floribunda' by the National Rose Society.

But by this time something else had happened. As a consequence of the influence of Victoria Sackville-West, and some lesser gardener journalists, 'old-fashioned' roses had been restored to favour in the gardens of the middle and upper classes. Middle-class people, following the example of the sophisticated rich and noble gardeners, sought for their gardens the old Bourbon, Provence, damask and musk roses, competed in collecting moss roses, and began also to plant the botanical species in their search for graceful simplicity, especially some Chinese species, such as the *rugosas*, and *R. moyesii*. It became almost a mark of ill-breeding to have floribunda roses in your garden, and even the hybrid teas were often lined out in the kitchen-garden to provide their incomparable flowers for cutting, without marring the orna-mental garden itself with the ugly rigidity of their bushes. But the cottagers, not to mention the by now much more numerous small suburban gardeners, were, as I have said, in a position at last to buy their own roses, especially when the cheap multiple stores, such as Woolworth's, began to package and offer them like any other branded, packaged merchandise. Thus the floribunda has turned out to be, in a sense, the first race of garden roses specifically for the cottage and small suburban gardener, who prefers it to the older roses. The population of floribunda roses in England must be comparable with the popu-lation of people, for numbers. The cottagers who love its mas-ses of bright flowers are the heirs to one of the most complex garden plants in the world of horticulture, with the sap of a dozen or more species of roses from all over the world, in its veins.

It is very unlikely that sophisticated rich gardeners will be able, ever again, to seek for 'old-fashioned' flowers in the gardens of working-class cottagers; however, they may still find them in the cottage gardens of the retired middle-class gardener, who has, perhaps, taken over the task of acting as museum curator for old cultivars.

SAFFRON WALDEN,
ESSEX
Cottage gardeners invented 'careless planting'; professionals took the style and made it sophisticated.

[10]
High Gardening

Because of its subsequent influence on millions of cottage gardens and small suburban gardens, it will now be necessary to give some account of the advances made in the age of what, on the analogue of 'high' farming, one may fairly call 'high' gardening, the period during which science and technology were first deliberately applied to horticulture on a grand scale. If one had to name one man as the prophet of this period of gardening history which enormously enlarged the garden flora as well as garden technology, that man would certainly have to be not John Claudius Loudon, as one might have expected, but Joseph Paxton; it was he who set the pace and style, just as Loudon accomplished the perhaps even more important social task of bringing the small householder to a full awareness of what modern horticulture could achieve for him.

Paxton was born to very poor parents in 1801; so the first garden he was conscious of, and perhaps worked in, must have been a small cottage garden. Somehow, the boy contrived to educate himself; the next thing we know about him is that in his early twenties he was working as a gardener in the Horticultural Society's experimental garden in Chiswick; and that, before his twenty-fifth birthday, he was put in charge of the society's arboretum there. But Paxton did not see for himself, in England, such a future as he wanted, for he was ambitious as well as very able; and he was planning to emigrate to America. But at this time he made the acquaintance of the Duke of Devonshire, who, being the society's Chiswick landlord, often visited their garden, to which he had his own private door. The Duke took a liking to young Paxton, often talked with him, conceived a respect for his brains and, finding himself without a head gardener for his great estate of Chatsworth just as he was about to go abroad for a time, offered the job to Paxton at £36 a year, plus a cottage. He can hardly have foreseen that the young

Literally a cottage garden, for it belonged to an estate cottage, the COTTAGE GARDEN SISSINGHURST, KENT, was deliberately planted with cottage flowers by V. Sackville-West in the style developed by Gertrude Jekyll.

gardener would turn him into one of the most enthusiastic gardening noblemen in the land, involve him in expense which might have given even a Duke of Devonshire pause, and make Chatsworth, whose garden had lately been running down and which Paxton found neglected, into a place of pilgrimage for gardeners from all over the world. Within twelve years of his appointment, Paxton had made Chatsworth both the most spectacular and the most famous garden in England, *the* garden of the new age of technology; at thirty-seven he was offered the head gardenership of Windsor Castle with a salary of £1,000 a year and refused it.

In his transformation of Chatsworth Paxton earned the approval of all but Loudon. He was wholeheartedly a scientific, even a mechanical gardener. He became, in the course of his gardening, an architect, a village planner and builder, a company director, a Member of Parliament, and the designer of that Exhibition Hall of steel and glass which subsequently became known as the Crystal Palace. I have read that the structural principle of that great building, forerun by the great greenhouse which he built at Chatsworth, was suggested to him by the structure of the leaf of the great Victoria amazonica water-lily. Paxton was knighted; he ceased to be a gardener; that left nothing for him to do, so he died. He made the most remarkable garden in the world by technical skill, industry, business management efficiency; and without taste. The gardens modelled on his style might, indeed they did, epater*; but what Paxton contributed to gardening lore was ingenious contrivance, a sort of horticultural engineering, and a number of new orchids.*[78]

Paxton gardens had enormous masses of colour made of the massed plantings of the largest and most flamboyant new hybrid plants; conservatories full of flaming tropical exotics; greenhouses producing tropical fruits better than they could be grown in the tropics. Technically, his gardens, and gardens made in his manner, were marvellous; aesthetically, they were not so good; and it is possible that some of the later reaction in favour of cottagey simplicities can be traced to him. But how did his work affect the cottage garden positively? Immediately, not at all, although it did change the look of the small suburban garden. But in the long run, because Paxton was the creator and prophet of modern gardening, forcing the pace of scientific investigation into plant life and behaviour, garden technology, garden machinery development, and the development of greenhouse building, he did, of course, bring about very great changes even in those small gardens which were so far beneath the scale on which he worked; we shall see something of this when we come to analyse the modern cottage garden.

Miles Hadfield has pointed out that garden tools and machinery were much advanced as a consequence of the great progress in the technology of iron founding and the manufacture of metals in general during the late eighteenth and early nineteenth centuries.[79] The first horticultural effect of these advances was on greenhouses:

A number of new designs were soon forthcoming and communicated to the Society; some were more ingenious than practical. Commercial production of greenhouses was stimulated. Birmingham firms manufacturing metallic and copper sashes were eager to make use of these improvements. Richard and Jones, 'patent metallic hothouse manufacturers', were early in the field; Thomas Clark, formerly of Jones and Clark, was soon leading it. His first orders, with working drawings, still exist. An engraving published in 1830 of a conservatory he built at The Grange, Hampshire, gives an idea of the developments that had taken place. Clark supplied hothouses to many of the great gardens of the day–eventually to the Queen at Osborne and Frogmore.

A number of the new designs were based on more scientific methods of trapping the sun. But the systems of artificial heating remained fundamentally unaltered. Heat was provided by fermentation beds, or by passing the products of combustion through a flue.[80]

But soon, not later than 1826, heating systems employing the circulation of steam and hot water through pipes were in use. Can this advance in the heating of plant houses have been the origin of central heating systems? I leave that to the social historians. Not until our own times was there, in electric heating and in the 'blue flame' type of paraffin stove, methods suitable for the heating of really small greenhouses; still, the principles were established in the greenhouses of the early and middle nineteenth century.

By far the most important mechanical advance–a machine ancestral to all the small garden cultivating machines now used in small as well as in large gardens–was Ferrabee's lawnmower, first mentioned in the *Gardeners' Magazine* in the year 1831. But this proto-lawnmower was improved on at once by another, the invention of a man named Budding who based its design on a machine used for cropping the pile on certain kinds of cloth manufactured in the north country mills. With his principles and features, Budding established those of the modern lawnmower of the cylinder type. Our cylinder mowers are improved in detail, but not in principle:

such mowers, cheapened by the mass production manu-facturing methods invented by Henry Ford, were at last at the disposal and within the reach, economically, of the cottager and suburban gardener, in our own century, putting lawns, hitherto mowed by the scythe–which calls for great skill–within the reach of the cottage and small suburban gardener. Budding patented his lawnmower; and in his account of what it would accomplish, he pointed out that among its advantages was that of being able to close-cut grass which, growing in the shade of trees, was too weak to stand against the scythe.

Another great advance which began in this epoch was in the methods and in the materials, but above all in the under-standing, of manuring garden soils. Animal and vegetable wastes and 'green manuring' crops (notably annual lupins) had been used for thousands of years to improve the fertility of garden soils. The Roman agronomist Columella, drawing heavily on the Carthaginian agronomist Mago, had had a remarkably sophisticated understanding of this problem. How did the gardeners and farmers of the ancient, non-scientific civilizations discover that plants fed with decaying organic matter grew better? They did not: the discovery was made much earlier than any civilization, in Neolithic times, and presumably by accident. At all events, gardeners and farmers knew that plants did benefit if the land was dressed with decaying wastes; but not how or why. But early in the century we are concerned with here, Sir Humphry Davy, by analysing plant tissues and manure tissues comparatively, discovered that there were elements common to both. Doubtless this seems obvious enough now; but he had established that the plants took something from the manures, and discovered what that something was, or a part of it.

Then the great German chemist Justus von Liebig went further. Discovering by means of a series of classic experi-ments how much carbon, nitrogen, calcium, phosphorus, sodium and potash were removed from a soil in the ordinary crop rotation of seeds used for hay, wheat, turnips and barley, he ascertained the principal mineral needs of a range of crop plants; and even the proportions of each mineral required by the several different crop plants he worked with. Later, two young Englishmen, J.B.Lawes, a farmer, and a chemist named J.H.Gilbert, began experimental work at Lawes's farm at Rothamsted, Harpenden, which became the world-famous Rothamsted Experimental Station; their work was aimed at discovering what proportions of what minerals

The jungle of flowers pressing about this half-timbered cottage at EAST HAGBOURNE, BERKSHIRE, looks as authentic as any of those humble rural plots recorded in Edwardian days by Helen Allingham. In fact the layout is Robinsonian and there are rareties in the profuse growth which reveal considerable sophistication.

were required by the principal crop plants; and at such things as the power of various kinds of soil to retain nutrient substances in diverse weather conditions. (It was left to our own epoch to discover the importance of the 'trace' elements, so-called because they are both present and required in minute traces only.) Gilbert, by treating animal bones and mineral phosphates with sulphuric acid, produced the first artificial fertilizer, superphosphate. Nitrogen fertilizer was supplied by importing guano from Peru; it is interesting in this context that this nitrogen-rich guano (sea-bird droppings accumulated in vast quantity on certain Peruvian islands) was not only used as manure by the pre-Inca and Inca farmers of ancient Peru, but its use was very carefully regulated and the birds responsible for it were rigorously protected by law. Guano continued to be the most important nitrogenous manure until von Liebig discovered how to 'fix' atmospheric nitrogen, a process for which mankind had until then depended solely on certain micro-organisms called azobacters, and thus made possible the manufacture of nitrates on a scale sufficient for agriculture and horticulture.

It was, then, in the first half of the nineteenth century that experimental farmers and gardeners, working with chemists, began the long work which has culminated in providing every cottage and suburban garden, as well as the world's farmers, with cheap and easily handled artificial fertilizers composed of the principal plant nutrient salts combined in various proportions according to the needs of particular crop or ornamental plants, and to the nature of the soil being tilled. And if modern experimental gardeners have discovered that these valuable aids, which have multiplied weight of crop per acre three or fourfold, are not themselves enough, and that the ancient organic manure materials are still required to maintain the texture and structure of soil in optimum condition for plant roots, it nevertheless remains true that good gardening has been made both very much easier and much more common by these means.

The field in which advances at the time in question were negligible was that of plant and garden pest and disease control: the great potato blight outbreak which decimated the population of Ireland because the Irish had become so dependent on this one garden and field crop that if it failed they were bound to starve, found the plant pathologists and the chemists completely helpless; and later in the century, when the aphis *Phylloxera vastatrix*, an American insect parasitic on the native American *Vites* which had developed

High Gardening

resistance to it, whereas the Old World vines had no resistance, attacked and nearly wiped out the European wine industry, the chemists and pathologists were unable to help; they had been equally helpless when, earlier, the vines were attacked by American fungus parasites. Farmers were still obliged to regard the blights which attacked their crops as acts of God which one could do nothing about; and gardeners great and small were in the same case when their fruit, vegetables and flowers were afflicted with diseases, or attacked by parasitic insects and micro-organisms. Not until our own times did gardeners have the means to control these pests and diseases.

Activity in the collecting of new plants and breeding or selecting new cultivars for gardens was intense throughout the whole century. We have seen how the example was set much earlier by men like the Tradescants, and plant collecting had continued on a slowly increasing scale since the sixteenth century; but now the pace became very much faster, and plants flooded into England from all over the world: during the eighteenth century about 500 new species were introduced to English gardens; in the next century the newcomers were counted in thousands. It had been known since Vancouver's voyage of discovery in 1791 that the north-west coast of America had a rich flora still unknown to science and to gardening; and Menzies, Vancouver's botanist, had brought home a great deal of herbarium material for study. Now, beginning in 1823 when the Horticultural Society sent David Douglas plant-collecting, first in the east of north America, then in the far west, a determined effort was made to bring home living plant material. Douglas enriched our gardens with new maples, mahonias and other shrubs, with many fine evergreen conifers, with such bulb flowers as *Camassia*, and such herbaceous perennials as the *Clarkia*, which was to become a 'typical' cottage flower; with Monkey Musk, *Nemophila*, *Garrya*, and with the flowering currant beloved of cottage gardeners.

Another flower which we think of as typically a 'cottage garden flower', and which is often grown in a pot on a windowsill – which, indeed, became almost a sentimental symbol of the cottage garden – had a curious career: *Mimulus moschatus*, commonly called musk. But it was quite a latecomer to our gardens and its career lasted little more than half a century.

David Douglas found it on the banks of the Columbia River in California, which he had reached by sea via Cape

Horn after a journey of nine months, in the year 1826. He liked the flower and sent home some seed; in his note on this find he says nothing about scent. It is possible that one of the plants from which he collected seed was scented, but certain that the plant is, typically, scentless. The seed which he sent home was germinated and the seedlings raised in the Horticultural Society's garden at Chiswick. At least two, probably more, of the seedlings had the characteristic strong but delicate scent of musk. One of these must have been the plant used by Professor John Lindley as the basis of his official scientific description of the new plant, for in that description he writes of it emitting 'a powerful odour of musk'. As a result he called the plant *Moschatus*, and it came to be accepted that the scent was a characteristic of the plant. Had Lindley been able to examine the plant in the wild, and in numerous specimens, he would have discovered that, typically, it has no scent. From another scented plant the Horticultural Society's gardeners propagated vegetatively – that is by cuttings – more plants, from which, again, cuttings were taken. So that the 'clone' which finally got into commerce was the scented musk.

I have never smelt a scented specimen of *M. moschatus*, for there has not been one in Britain during my lifetime. But it must have been an exceptionally delicious scent for the plant quickly became very popular with all classes of gardeners, and especially with cottage gardeners; and it has very little but its scent to recommend it.

The scent is supposed to have vanished suddenly and universally in the year 1912 or 1913. Of course, it did nothing of the kind; it had long been waning, and this waning was noticed as early as 1880. But the press made a story of the sudden vanishing of the musk scent. The most idiotic theories were put forward to explain this strange behaviour; the only theories not attended to were those of botanists who knew quite well what the truth was. Typically, as I have said, a scentless plant, it produces, rarely, a scented mutant: the Horticultural Society's seed, or rather some of it, clearly came from one such plant. The scent persisted, of course, in the vegetatively propagated plants. But, as soon as nurserymen and amateur gardeners began to grow the plants from seed taken from parent plants whose flowers had been pollinated from scentless plants, the scent began to fade. Until, at last, slowly but inevitably, it was bred out entirely.

Implicit in this explanation of the vanishing scent of musk is the hope that it is not lost for ever. Somewhere in the world's

Preceding pages Cottage garden topiary can sometimes take over the front gardens of a whole village street as here at CHIPPING CAMPDEN, GLOUCESTERSHIRE, where columns of giant girth, an unsteady cock and monstrously swollen, smooth hedges create an atmosphere of dream.

[148]

population of *M. moschatus* plants the gene for scent is still there: but we shall need a stroke of luck equal to the last one, a chance in many millions, to bring that scent out again.

Meanwhile in the early nineteenth century other collectors were working in Brazil, Chile and Peru. From 1812 to 1831, John Reeves, an East India Company inspector in China, with a fine garden of his own in Macao, was sending Chinese cultivars from Chinese to English gardens: from him we have chrysanthemums, peonies, camellias and azaleas; Reeves's chrysanthemums have been favourite cottage flowers for a century. For stocking the great hot-houses of this age of high gardening, the Horticultural Society's collector Karl Hartweg spent six years in Central America, sending home orchids, cacti and the seeds of trees, especially the Mexican pines.

When Captain Cook's ship *Resolution* sailed out of Plymouth in June 1772, she had on board one Francis Masson, commissioned by the great Sir Joseph Banks to collect plants for the Royal Gardens at Kew, at the Cape of Good Hope, where Cook landed his passenger before sailing on towards the south and the discovery of Australia. Masson sent or took back to England more than fifty species of *Pelargonium*, in due course to become the favourite plant for cottage windowsills and suburban garden bedding-out schemes. From the Canary Islands, where he collected on his way back to England and in a special expedition to those islands, and Madeira, Masson sent home the seeds which were the origin of the garden *Cinerarias* (the genus is *Senecio*; *Cineraria*, like *Syringa* and other garden names for plants, is a misnomer). He introduced many of the Cape Heaths, which became favourite greenhouse and house plants. He brought us the *Ixias* which have naturalized in an area of west Scotland. Some of Masson's plant collecting in the Cape was done in the company of the famous Swedish botanist von Thunberg, who was also sending plants home to Europe. Masson, after a return to England and his expedition to Portugal and the Atlantic islands, was back at the Cape in 1785, preparing a garden where he could establish his collected plants before sending live material back to Kew: from him we got the lovely *Nerines*, the strange *Stapelias*, *Massonias*–in all he introduced about 400 species new to English botanists and gardeners; since most of them were tender or half-hardy, only a relatively small number became cottage garden flowers.

Masson was followed at the Cape by William J. Burchell, who collected herbarium material for Kew between 1810 and 1815; he may also have sent home living bulbs and seeds, although since that was not his job there is no record of it. Who sent or brought home to us such other South African flowers as *Watsonia*, *Schizostylis*, *Dierama*, *Phygelius*, *Gazania*, *Agapanthus* and many more? Most of them perhaps reached us by way of Holland. *Agapanthus* has been grown in England since 1753; *Streptocarpus rexii* first flowered in England in 1823; *Clivias* a few years later.

South African species of *Gladiolus*, of which there are many more than anywhere else in the world, reached England early in the nineteenth century and cross-breeding began so soon that there were garden hybrids as early as 1823. But the huge showy ones, so popular for late summer display in cottage and suburban gardens, were bred from South African species in Holland, the first of the new cultivars reaching us in about 1840. So this flower, now to be seen in millions of cottage and suburban gardens, was unknown in them until the second half of the nineteenth century, and probably rare until about 1870.

Such difficult South African genera as *Disa* and *Protea* have no place in cottage gardens; but the arum lilies, *Zantedeschia*, for long cultivated only as greenhouse plants, became very much cottage garden flowers in the south-west and old clumps of them can be seen in hundreds of Devonshire village gardens. These were only the white arums; the yellow and pink ones were not tried in England until the end of the century.

David Douglas was not, of course, the only man to collect plants in North America. Frazer was sending home azaleas and rhododendrons about the turn of the century, including *Rhododendron catawbiense*, an ancestor of very many garden hybrids. Japanese cultivars and wild plants were being introduced to Holland, whence they soon reached us, by Philip von Siebold, a Prussian aristocrat and a very great plantsman, between 1823 and 1830. Less than two decades later, Joseph Dalton Hooker, later to succeed his father as Director of Kew Gardens, was sending home the magnificent Himalayan and Sikhimese rhododendrons. The nursery firm of Veitch, probably responsible for more good plant introductions than any other agency, had Lobb collecting for them in Chile as early as 1840.

Robert Fortune sent home a great number of beautiful new plants from China between 1840 and 1850, and from Japan in the 1860s. Fortune worked at first for the Horticultural Society, later for the United States Government. Also in the 1850s John Jeffrey was plant collecting for a Scottish syn-

An unpremeditated yet delightfully decorative instance at KNUTSFORD, CHESHIRE, of the cottage garden tradition of the mingling of flowers and the essential vegetable.

dicate, in California, and Lobb was back in Chile on a second expedition. A little later John Gould Veitch, of the nursery firm already named, went personally to Japan to bring back good plants which had been overlooked. Some plant collectors, some of them even more successful than these – Farrer, Augustine Henry, Wilson the greatest of them all, Kingdon Ward, were yet to come; but here we are concerned with the early and mid century, the age of 'high' gardening.

Some of the most familiar cottage garden plants began to be seen in such gardens for the first time in this epoch. I have mentioned the big gladiolus, a newcomer then, although it is now quite difficult to imagine a small cottage or suburban garden without it. Dahlias were first introduced from Mexican into Spanish gardens in the year 1789, reached France in 1802, and England (Chelsea Physic Garden) in 1803. But the great range of modern garden dahlias are all derived from a parcel of dahlia seed, whose seedlings proved extremely variable, imported from France in 1815. Owing to the successive fashions for different forms of dahlia, there was the usual drift of the older forms from the gardens of the rich into the cottage gardens. In the case of this so very variable flower, fashion changes were so quick that the newcomer reached the small gardens quite soon; yet it was not until relatively late in the century that the dahlia became familiar in the autumnal cottage garden and the gardens of the new suburban sprawl.

One has only to think of dahlias in cottage gardens to think also of the equally important autumn-flowering chrysanthemums; they have, although it is difficult to realize it, been in cottage gardens no longer than the dahlias. They were very ancient cultivars in Chinese gardens; they had already been created out of wild species at least as early as 500 BC; in fact they are so ancient as man-made plants, that their wild ancestors can no longer be determined. Their first introduction into Europe was to Holland in 1688, a year when the English were busy with other matters than gardens. That introduction was from Japan, to whose gardeners these flowers had been introduced, by way of Korea, about AD 800.[81] Japanese gardeners changed the shape of chrysanthemum flowers considerably, preferring the less formal flower heads to the Chinese incurved, stylized varieties. The 1688 introduction failed. Not until a century later did a seaman, Captain Blanchard, bring another consignment of chrysanthemum cultivars, this time from China, to Marseilles, in 1789, oddly enough the year of the introduction of the dahlia into Spain. Blanchard's plants established themselves, and rooted cuttings taken from them reached England in 1795. By 1808, eight Chinese chrysanthemums were being grown here.[82] The Horticultural Society, at the time being steered by Sabine, one of its most vigorous secretaries, took a particular interest in these plants, and in 1823 introduced other varieties from China; again, in 1843, they asked Fortune, who was collecting for them in China, to send home more chrysanthemums. At this point a gifted breeder of garden plants, John Salter, took up the genus. In about 1860 Fortune, by then in Japan, sent home still more chrysanthemum cultivars, introduced the Japanese flower shapes which, as I have said, differed greatly from the Chinese, and were, at first, far from popular.

So, then, the autumn flowering Far Eastern chrysanthemums, which had been the glory of Chinese gardens for more than 2,000 years, and which are now so essential a feature of our own cottage and suburban gardens and our most important florists' flower, were virtually unknown here until the middle of the nineteenth century and remained unfamiliar for at least another decade.

We can take yet another case of a thoroughly 'cottagey' flower; the perennial asters known as Michaelmas daisies began to reach England as early as 1633; that was the species later named *Aster tradescantii*. But most of the cultivars we are familiar with were products of nineteenth-century nursery work, and as for the very popular dwarf forms, the first appeared in the 1830s and did not reach their present perfection until the 1930s.

I asked a dozen acquaintances to name some 'typical' cottage garden flowers; among those not already dealt with in one of the earlier chapters, or above, three were mentioned: tobacco plants (*Nicotiana*); the scarlet salvia; and the red-hot poker, *Kniphophia*. Two of the latter were eighteenth-century introductions and might, I suppose, have reached the smaller gardens by 1800, although they can hardly have been common: the rest of the species were not introduced until after 1870 and were in any case tender. Most of the *Nicotiana* species were nineteenth-century introductions, and it is very unlikely that any cultivar had reached the cottage garden or the small suburban garden before 1830. The *Salvia* reached England in 1772, but cannot have been widely enough distributed to begin marring our small gardens until the beginning of the next century.

Sweet peas are associated in the public mind with pretty cottages and the little gardens of the suburbs; and for long

they have constituted one of the more important 'classes' in village flower shows. They date from the early eighteenth-century, but not as we know them. It was in 1699 that a priest, Father Cupani, sent the first batch of *Lathyrus odorata* seed to reach us, to a Dr Uvedale of Enfield. The plant, although a native of southern Italy and Sicily, was certainly unknown here before 1700.

The flowers of these early plants were purple, pale purple and red, or white and red. Comparatively little change in type or range of colour occured for a long time, but self-coloured forms were raised, and one was given an award by the Royal Horticultural Society in 1865.[83]

Serious breeding by crossing did not even begin until 1870; and the kinds of sweet pea we know now, quite different in shape of flower, number of flowers per stem, and other particulars, did not emerge from the breeders' hands until after 1900. As for the earlier, original type from Cupani's seeds, how long would it have taken for them to become so widely distributed that even cottagers might grow some? If we assume that all the seed ultimately in circulation could be traced back to Dr Uvedale's original planting of sweet peas, half a century is hardly too long. At all events, one can safely say that sweet peas had never been heard of in cottage gardens before 1750, although the native *Lathyrus*, the everlasting pea, a perennial, was an old inhabitant of the small garden.

Some other introductions of this age of 'high' gardening have managed to become 'typical cottage flowers': *Anemone japonica* was first introduced by Fortune in 1845; allowing adequate time for propagation, distribution and cheapening, the Japanese anemones may perhaps have been in some cottage gardens by 1875. Lupins (the perennials, not the ancient annual lupins, of course) were brought in by John Tradescant in 1637 and were probably fairly common in small gardens, in the blue form only, a century later, for their yield of seed is very large. But the lupins we are familiar with, the great spikes of diversely bicoloured flowers, were first bred by George Russel, a Yorkshireman, in his cottage garden, in 1937, three centuries after Tradescant's introduction. Phlox, an eighteenth-century newcomer, may have got into the cottage garden by, say, 1775, but the garden cultivars were not put into commerce until our own time. The big 'show' pansies came into the cottage and small suburban garden in mid nineteenth century; but the very familiar and very 'cottagey' violas only a quarter of a century later.[84]

The cock in box at BROADCLYST, DEVONSHIRE, overwhelming the small garden with its gargantuan presence, is a superb example of the survival of the seventeenth-century mania for wildly extravagant topiary.

Plant collectors might have braved the Himalayan and Andean snows in vain, and the work of the plant breeder been all *ars gratis artis* had it not been for the coincident growth of a nursery trade to propagate and distribute the new garden plants; and, incidentally, to take a very important part in the making of them. Of the many new nurseries, the most important from the point of view of the new small gardener were those placed near to the new suburbs, the streets of little houses creeping out from great urban centres all over England, invading the countryside. Not quite typical, perhaps, since Loudon thought it exceptionally good, was the firm of John Pope & Son of Handsworth near Birmingham.[85] John Pope himself had been plant collecting in North America; and as well as the more or less familiar herbaceous perennials, he had a stock of more than a hundred rarities. In the late 1830s the firm carried out an important experiment to test the hardiness of allegedly tender plants. The hardiness of *Camellia japonica* was thoroughly established, yet this discovery made very little impression on practical gardeners in general. Pope also established the hardiness of *Magnolia grandiflora*, which was thereafter widely planted, but it was not, of course, ever a cottage garden tree. The firm of Pope and many others now specialized in ornamentals, but yet others were specializing in fruit and some of them made an attempt to get order out of the chaos into which fruit tree nomenclature had fallen. Ronalds of Brentford were forward in this work, and their 1931 catalogue, illustrated with colour plates painted by Ronald's daughter Elizabeth, described 179 varieties of tree fruits.[86] One nurseryman tried to cut the Gordian knot of confusion in fruit tree nomenclature – there were varieties with as many as fifteen different local names – by planting specimens of every distinct variety in a single six-acre orchard, totally ignoring the old names, and renaming all of them: this was, needless to say, an heroic failure.

Drystone walling, characteristic of the Yorkshire setting of KIRKBY MALHAM marries well with a battlemented hedge and a crude topiary peacock.

Following the example set by Kew, botanic gardens for the scientific study of plants, but also for the edification of the amateur and professional gardener, were improved or founded in several parts of the country. William McNab, the Kew-trained curator of the Edinburgh Botanic Garden, in 1820 moved the entire collection to its present, then new, site; and incidentally landscaped the grounds with sure taste.[87] In 1838 David Moore, the Dublin garden's greatest curator, succeeded Ninian Nairn at the Irish National Botanic Garden, Glasnevin, and made important changes and

High Gardening

improvements.[88] The Liverpool Botanic Garden was founded in 1803 and by the 1820s was receiving thousands of gardener visitors. In 1831 Loudon designed a botanic garden for the Birmingham Botanical and Horticultural Society and in the same year Cambridge University Botanic Garden was moved to a much larger ground. In Glasgow, William Jackson Hooker was making the small Glasgow Botanic Garden, attached to the university, famous and there were new gardens of the same kind–horticultural, botanical–started in Bury St Edmunds, Hull and some other towns.[89]

Thus, between the first and last decades of the nineteenth century the science of gardening was very much advanced, even if the art of garden design suffered from the vulgarity of an age, with a superabundance of energy, although towards the end of the century new men and women came forward to correct the excesses which were due to the excitement of new plant material, new techniques, and new machines. The effect of scientific gardening on the small suburban garden was more or less immediate; on the country cottage garden, much less so; it served, as it had for so long, as a conservatory of the simplicities.

11

The Cottage Garden
and
National Economy

The law locks up both man and woman
Who steals a goose from off a common,
But lets the greater felon loose
Who steals the common from the goose.
Or you may prefer the version:
The fault is great in man or woman
Who steals the goose from off the common
But what can plead that man's excuse
Who steals the common from the goose?

The second version is from the *Tickler's Magazine* (February 1821); the other may be older. What rustic genius wrote it is unknown; perhaps he was no rustic, but what J.C.Squire once described as one of those 'people who write in private what in public they allege to be folk-songs'. There are other versions, and all of them refer to the same gigantic crime, by far the grandest larceny in England's history: between 1760 and 1867 England's small class of rich men, using as their instrument Acts of the Parliament which they controlled through a tiny and partly bought and paid for electorate, stole seven million acres of common land, the property and the livelihood of the common people of England. The excuse most commonly offered in justification of this monstrous theft is that only by enclosure could farming by the new methods be made efficient and profitable. That is now questionable, but two things are certain, that the world is faced with mass starvation in the not very distant future because the criterion £sd-returns per man-hour-acre has replaced the criterion food-returns per man-hour-acre; and that the English cottager, who formerly had his four-acre garden and his common grazing rights, by losing the essential latter, lost his freedom with his livelihood.

There is a widely accepted delusion that very large-scale agriculture is more 'efficient' than small-scale cottage or peasant agriculture. This persists in the face of the evidence,

Cottage gardens such as this one at SPAUNTON, YORKSHIRE, contribute not only vegetables and fruit but eggs and poultry to the national economy.

even scientific evidence. I will come to that presently. The truth is that by 'industrializing' agriculture and horticulture, big money profits can be made, but only at the expense of food production; to the best of my knowledge, it is impossible to stay alive by eating dollar bills or one-pound notes, or even ten-pound notes.

I have referred in one of the foregoing chapters to a conversation recorded in his diary by Lord Torrington with Humphry Repton at an inn where both were staying. Repton admired the way in which, in a neighbouring county, cottagers were being 'given' (of the land which was immemorially the people's) four-acre plots (harking back to the normal cottager's holding in the reign of Elizabeth I) by way of compensation for the grazing rights which had been stolen from them by the Enclosure Acts. It will be recalled that Torrington had pointed out that whereas the old rights had been inalienable, the cottager with alienable land was perfectly free to beggar himself and his family by selling his little bit of land for some temporary and ephemeral gain, or in an emergency.

The Acts of Enclosure did, in fact, provide for cottagers to be compensated for loss of their ancient rights by being provided with gardens, or what were called garden allotments, later allotment gardens, of several acres. But since the cottagers often did not know what rights they might claim, just as so many of the poor of today do not know what help Parliament has voted them in return for what Parliament has stolen from them, what was to compel the enclosing landlord to give them anything at all? Robbed by the grand larceny of Parliament, the cottagers were cheated by the petty larceny of landlords; for example, between 1845 and 1867 half a million acres were enclosed, but only just over 2,000 were set aside as allotment gardens.

As a result of their new misery, that ugly poverty reflected in the difference between the living conditions of Old Sally and her husband Dick, in Larkrise, and those of their neighbours, many more country cottagers than the gentry and burgesses had bargained for flocked into the towns seeking work. Naturally, the industrial burgesses wanted the lowest possible wage levels; and that, then as now, meant that they must contrive as large a pool of unemployed as possible, for they had not read or were unimpressed by Adam Smith's argument that it was in their own interests to pay high wages so as to create a market for their goods; as unimpressed as they were by the spectacle of starving

women and children. It became necessary, if agriculture was
not to be ruined for want of labour, to find an inducement to
keep cottagers in the country and working on the farms, but
to do this without substantially raising their wages, for that
would mean raising food prices, and that would entail either
worse starvation in the towns, or raising industrial wages and
so reducing industrial profits.

So, beginning in 1819, a whole series of Acts of Parliament
were passed to require local authorities to provide cottagers
with allotment gardens big enough to enable them to raise
vegetable and fruit crops which would help to feed their
families; but not so big that they could get a living off them
and so afford to stop working for a farmer. These Acts were
not quite ineffectual: for example, following the Act of 1894,
during the next four years 32,000 allotment gardeners
received a total of 15,000 acres of land. All the Acts between
1814 and the end of the century were consolidated in the Small-
holding and Allotments Act of 1908, by which, in the section
concerned with allotments, local authorities were not only
empowered but required to make provision for allotments.

Before that date, allotment societies and allotment co-opera-
tives had already become quite numerous and important. In
1842, for example, G. B. Lawes, of Rothamsted fame, had
organized a model one at Harpenden in Hertfordshire. But
there were earlier associations of the same kind, and in time
they became so successful that some of the Acts of Parliament
empowered local authorities to deal with them as recognized
responsible bodies.

Allotment gardens (by law they are not identical with
allotments) were a very important addition to the cottage and
small suburban garden. The gardener could give more of his
house plot to flowers, and raise his vegetables, or even keep
his chickens and, perhaps, rabbits, on the allotment. Not
that it always worked out like that, and during the First
World War, when allotment and allotment garden holders
made a substantial contribution to the national food supply,
ornamentals almost vanished from the cottage garden; even
the rich were ploughing up their lawns to grow potatoes. At
the end of that war there were 1,330,000 being cultivated,
and since the rate of decline in the number was slow and it
was obvious that a majority of allotment and allotment garden
holders wanted to keep their plots, new legislation became
necessary.[90]

In the Allotments Act of 1922, an allotment garden is
defined as: '... an allotment not exceeding 40 poles in extent

English Cottage Gardens

which is wholly or mainly cultivated by the occupier for the production of vegetable and fruit crops for consumption by himself and his family'.[91] This means that an allotment garden must not exceed a quarter of an acre. By the same Act, borough, urban and district and parish councils are under a statutory obligation to provide allotment gardens for all suitable persons, provided the application is made by six registered parliamentary electors or six ratepayers. The same authorities were given powers of compulsion to acquire land either by rent or purchase.

Land purchased for allotment gardens by local authorities offers the best security of tenure. If purchased under the Allotments Acts it cannot be used for any other purpose without the permission of the Ministry of Agriculture. When they are town planned and the scheme reaches its final stages, similar security is obtained. All plots however acquired are usually let to tenants on a yearly agreement, terminable by either party giving six months notice to the other.

That is an extract from the Royal Horticultural Society's *Dictionary of Gardening*. It is notable that no move has ever been made to return the land to the people; that could only have been done by an act of expropriatory nationalization, that is, an exact reverse of the eighteenth- and nineteenth-century acts of expropriatory de-nationalization. Rent is always exacted for allotments and allotment gardens.

In the Second World War the number of allotments under cultivation increased to a million and three quarters; and although the total fell after the war, it was still above 800,000, and in the early 1960s allotment gardens were making a very considerable contribution to the feeding of three to four million people.

Is it possible to arrive at an estimate of the contribution made towards the national larder by cottage and suburban gardeners from their gardens and allotment gardens? It is, and the result is surprising. In 1956 Wye College, the agriculture and horticultural college of London University, and one of the world's leading institutions in the study and teaching of scientific gardening, carried out a survey which revealed a most unexpected state of affairs. The Report, published by R.H.Best and J.T.Ward, was called *The Garden Controversy*; the title, and the authors' approach to their subject, derived from the dispute between those who favoured high-density housing as a means of saving farmland from urban encroachment and those who wanted low-density housing in the interests of amenity. The survey showed,

At both
NUTHAMPSTEAD BURY HERTFORDSHIRE (*left*) and KNAPTON, NORFOLK, the old art of the English cottage garden lives on in the combination of useful and ornamental elements.

The Cottage Garden and National Economy

among many other things, that garden activity declines in proportion to the density of housing; and as it also showed very clearly that cottage and suburban and council house gardens are not less but more efficient food producers than farms or market gardens, the authors claimed that the save-the-farmland-and-so-save-imports argument in favour of high-density housing was void.

Earlier surveys had established some of the data on which Wye's researchers based some of their calculations. For example, the proportions of households with any kind of cultivated gardens, varying very widely from one part of the country to another. Here is the table:

Region		Region	
South-east	75%	Midlands	47%
Wales	68%	North Midlands	44%
South	60%	North	34%
East	60%	North-east	25%
South-west	52%	North-west	11%
London	47% (*excluding Central London*)		

The year was 1944; demographic changes will have altered the figures, but hardly the proportions.

The researchers also used the figures established by Professor Dudley Stamp and published in his *The Land of Britain – Its Use and Misuse* (1948), of the proportion of land

cultivated by gardeners on a number of housing estates chosen as being representative. The extreme figures were 15·4 and 9·3 per cent. Stamp was able to estimate the production of food in small gardens and allotment gardens at a million and a quarter tons per annum; but that was in a war year; in peacetime the figure is substantially lower. But Stamp's work also made it possible to compare the output of food from gardens with that of food from farms, where both were growing the same crops. This is particularly interesting in our context; here is an extract from the table:

Yields per acre in tons from:	Farms	Gardens
Potatoes	7·0	6·9
Broad beans	3·5	3·7
Runner beans	4·0	4·2
Beetroot	9·4	11·5
Broccoli and cauliflower	5·8	4·6
Brussels sprouts	3·2	2·9
Cabbages	9·0	10·0
Carrots	12·0	10·4
Celery	10·9	8·9
Leeks	8·0	8·0
Lettuce	6·0	6·0
Onions	4·7	4·7
Parsnips	11·0	8·9
Turnips	10·2	7·8

In most of the crops the gardener, albeit an amateur, is a more efficient food producer than the farmer where garden crops are concerned; and, taking the totals, he grows 7·1 tons of food per acre to the 6·3 tons of the farmer. One might conclude that by taking away from the people seven million acres of land and handing it over to the landlords who let it to tenants, Parliament had achieved the startling result of robbing the nation of over five million tons of food per annum. Of course, the truth is not so simple; open-field agriculture and the use of commons for grazing were not gardening. The gardener scores every time by reason of the intensity of his cultivation. But my object is to emphasize a point which is not questionable: in terms of food per acre produced, the cottage gardener is more valuable to the nation than the farmer; and, as I shall show, there is quite overwhelming evidence that this is true, provided, that is, that one uses the economist's terms of reference and not those of a Food and Agriculture Organization prophet, or those which I myself used in *Soil and Civilization*, or that Massingham and I used in *Prophecy of Famine*, which, incidentally, was published about a decade before the pundits would admit the truth about the future world food situation.

To ascertain as nearly as possible the output of food grown by gardeners per household-acre, during the 1950s the Ministry of Food carried out a series of surveys by the sampling method. Several thousand households in representative rural and urban parts of the country took part in this work; and both weight of food grown, and its value at the ruling retail prices, were recorded. The figure reached was £67 10s. There has been some decline in vegetable growing by amateur gardeners since then, and some increase in prices, the latter factor being the greater. Perhaps the figure for today would not be much different. It is worth remarking in passing that, during the Second World War, the proportion of vegetables and fruit consumed in urban, working-class households which was home-grown was surprisingly high: in no quarter of the year was it lower than 10 per cent of the total; and in the third quarter of each year

A cottage gardener at NEWTON, CAMBRIDGESHIRE, resorts to age-old methods to keep birds off the cabbages – and off the caterpillars!

it rose as high as 25 per cent. These figures have little bearing on the present day; we are at peace, the worker's real wage has risen steeply, and the habit of consuming quick-frozen vegetables has become firmly established, leading to a fall in the growing of vegetables; the working class tends to become *embourgeoisé*. But we are here as much interested in what *can* be done by the cottage and suburban gardener as in what actually *is* done.

Another group of data used by the Wye College research workers was the result of an investigation into the use of gardens for food production, made by the Ministry of Agriculture's Land Service Research Group in 1951 and repeated in 1953. Here, extracted from one of the tables in the report, are some figures comparing garden use on suburban London Council housing estates–relatively high density housing–with that on private, relatively low density, housing estates: or not to be mealy-mouthed about it, the comparison is between working-class and lower middle-class gardens:

	Working class	Lower middle class
(1) Lawns, flowers, shrubs	29%	46%
(2) Paths and drives	17%	19%
(3) House	19%	20%
(4) Fruit and vegetables	21%	9%
(5) Sheds and garages	3%	3%
(6) Derelict	11%	3%

The significant lines for our context are (1) and (4). A point which I have repeatedly made for the past would seem to be still valid for the present: the use, and therefore the shape and flora, of the small garden depends on the gardener's wage.

We will return, for a moment, specifically to allotments and allotment gardens. In the mid 1950s Mr T.L.Ashton carried out for the municipal authorities of Keighley in Yorkshire a variety and productivity trial on an allotment of average size–ten rods (300 square yards). From this plot Ashton produced:

$224\frac{1}{4}$ lb of peas $268\frac{1}{2}$ lb of onions
 77 lb of beans   525 lb of cabbage, etc.
 92 lb of carrots   150 lb of cauliflower
 94 lb of beets   150 lb of brussels sprouts

That is, three quarters of a ton of food. There are fourteen ten-rod allotments to an acre, so we get an output of ten and a half tons per acre. But Ashton was an expert and his plot was correctly manured and cultivated; we can hardly put the average output per acre at more than eight tons. The Wye College survey, using these and other sources, estimated the

At SIBTON, SUFFOLK, where the pargework suggests the skeletal forms of the cabbages grown in the garden, the cottager is pursuing a long tradition of contribution to the national economy by using his plot chiefly for vegetables.

value of food crops from allotments alone, that is excluding the house plot gardens, at £24 million. Since then prices have risen, but on the other hand cottage and council house vegetable-growing has declined.

Comparative figures are, in the context of this chapter, of more interest than absolute figures: the survey made of comparison between garden and farm production of food crops in terms of money value; I will quote a short passage of the Report (*The Garden Controversy*) because it makes clear what, exactly, the survey was trying to discover:

Gardens and allotments are almost wholly limited to the production of vegetables, fruit (mainly soft) and flowers, with some small livestock products. Within agriculture only market gardens grow a similar selection of products, while farms generally produce the more basic commodities, such as cereals, milk, meat and other livestock products.

It is, therefore, sometimes suggested that the output of market gardens should be used in this type of comparison. The

Even such uncertainly rooted cottagers as this one at LITTLE WALDEN, ESSEX, will grow a bit of salad in improvized frames . . .

The Cottage Garden and National Economy

relative merits of domestic and agricultural food production are not being argued in vacuo, *however, but in relation to losses of agricultural land due to urban development. Only in a limited number of cases does this development take place on land devoted to market gardens. New development is, on the whole, occuring and is likely to occur, on better-than-average farmland, and for this reason it is an estimate of the average output from this type of land which we shall normally use for purposes of general comparison.*

It should here be borne in mind that when *residential* urban development encroaches on farmland, i.e. when such land is taken only for housing estates, 14 per cent of the land remains viable, as gardens, for the production of food crops. When the development is for general urban use, i.e. when it includes factories and other non-residential buildings, then the figures must be reduced to only 7 per cent.

There are some difficulties in comparing farm and garden production: they are summed up in *The Garden Controversy*:   . . . and a few flowers.

English Cottage Gardens

Vegetables produced in the garden are available for immediate consumption and, incidentally, have the great advantage of being completely fresh. The housewife growing her own vegetables is clearly saving the retail price of food she would otherwise have to buy at the local shop, and it is therefore logical to value garden output at retail prices. The position is different in the case of food produced on the farm which has to be marketed before it is available for consumption. Marketing is much more complex than is generally realized: it is a highly organized and costly process which employs a far larger proportion of the country's resources than is usually appreciated. The costs of marketing may well amount to as much as the costs of production on the farm; this is reflected by the fact that farm-gate prices are on average some 40 to 50 per cent below retail prices. Some of these costs are 'fixed costs' in the sense that, within limits, they will not vary greatly whatever the volume of trade; but others, notably those of transport and labour, which form a large proportion of total costs, do vary with the amount of produce handled. There would have to be a marked increase in these services, and hence in real costs to the community, if production from gardens were limited and much of the food lost had to be replaced from farms. The converse of this is to say that the production of food in domestic gardens leaves free for employment elsewhere resources which would otherwise be required in the distributive trades. This saving is likely to be considerable as production from gardens forms a substantial proportion of the total supplies of fruit and vegetables, especially during the summer and autumn months.

For these and supporting reasons it was found most nearly fair and sound to compare farm-gate prices of farm produce with the retail prices of garden produce. The year in question below is 1954–5, but as the figures are comparative, that is not significant.

The gross average farm-gate price for the output of all types of farmland in England and Wales was found to be £36 per cultivated acre. But the figure was about 25 per cent higher for the kind of land used for housing estates, suburban or sub-rural; so the sum of £45 was taken as being more nearly correct for purposes of comparison with garden productivity. Now the retail value of garden food crops per acre cultivated was found to be £300. If we load the comparison heavily in favour of the farm by using an equivalent of farm-gate prices for this garden produce, even that comes to £150 to be compared with £45. What is particularly interesting is that even the market garden figure is only £110.

Twentieth-century cottages at DEBDEN, ESSEX, set on a bank transformed into rock gardens bright with stone crop and saxifrage but never till now associated with East Anglian cottage plots.

The Cottage Garden and National Economy

These comparisons are made purely on an acre for cultivated acre basis; but if we are thinking of how much food a housing estate produces compared with the farmland it replaces, a new set of calculations become necessary. If only 14 per cent of a housing estate is cultivated for food crops, then the value of production per house-plot acre is about £42. This should be contrasted with the figure already given for the average value of gross output when the same area of land was used entirely for agricultural purposes, i.e. £45 for better than average farmland. In this case therefore garden productivity seems to be approximately the same as that for the more general types of farmland.

What conclusions can fairly be drawn from this? Well, they are obvious: surprising though it may seem, output of food from an acre of land covered with houses and small

Left A cottager at PORLOCK WEIR, SOMERSET, has managed to transform even this unpropitious stony soil into orderly rows of vegetables. *Right* An allotment at LITTLE SHELFORD, CAMBRIDGESHIRE, given over principally to potatoes. The allotment came into being as a way of compensating the 'peasant' for the loss of his common land to enclosure.

English Cottage Gardens

gardens–virtually 'cottage' gardens–at the usual working-class housing estate density, is almost equal to that from an acre of the best farmland entirely given over to the plough; and sensibly better than that from an acre of average quality farmland. *The Garden Controversy* points out that if you take the costs of production into account, the comparison is even more favourable to gardens; and that if the price subsidies given for the major farm crops but not for garden crops are also taken into the reckoning, the comparison would be, again, yet more favourable to the garden.

I have already said that, given the world food situation, with the threat of serious shortages becoming worse and worse as population increase overtakes food production increase, I object to the use of money values as a measure of food productivity. The reason for this objection is as follows: the economists assume that what matters is the money value of the crop produced from land because the pound sterling you save by growing a crop at home can be spent on importing such staples as meat and cereals. At present this is true; but for how long will it remain so? Suppose it to become untrue, then the only sound way of measuring output from land would be in food-value per man-hour-acre, not in money value: the money return from an acre of tomatoes is much greater than that from an acre of wheat, but we cannot live on tomatoes.

But economists are not thinking in those global terms; the context of the argument is the actual situation at this moment, that is one in which we are able to buy staple foods, cereals and meat overseas. That being so, the money measure is perfectly valid, and indeed preferable, since what matters is reducing the cost of our imports in £sd. So every pound we save by growing cabbages and beans at home can be spent on grain and meat abroad. Now connect that with the paragraph above and, making the point as sharply clear as we can, carrying the Wye survey result to its logical conclusion, we get this: that if every acre of farmland still left in Britain were to be covered with working-class housing estates at the average density for such estates, and given that the tenants of all those houses are obliged to cultivate their gardens for food crops, the net loss of output of food measured in money value would be nil; and there might be a small net gain. Startling, is it not?

However, let us draw some sensible instead of merely logical conclusions. The cottage, housing estate and suburban gardener's contribution to the national larder and so to our

Apple gathering at WHITTLESFORD, CAMBRIDGESHIRE, a region where fruit trees have always played an important role in cottage economy.

The Cottage Garden and National Economy

economy is a valuable one. Since about 66 per cent of English and Welsh households have a garden of some kind, or an allotment garden, and there are at least eleven million households, that contribution is coming from seven and a third million units. In 1956 the money value of the annual food crop from each was £5 12s 8d. In 1970, taking price increase into account, it can hardly be less than £7. Even making a guessed allowance for decline in vegetable and fruit growing in small gardens, the annual gain to the economy, the annual contribution to the balance of payments battle, can hardly be much less than £50 million. In short, cottage gardening is one of our major import-saving industries. Moreover, as urban development encroaches every year more and more on to farmland, it cannot but become increasingly important.

Left A sophisticated interpretation of the cottage garden at SAFFRON WALDEN, ESSEX, includes a classical image which whimsically relates it to the gardens of Imperial Rome.

The small cheap greenhouse is a twentieth-century development and makes this cottage gardener at AIRTON, YORKSHIRE, his own nurseryman.

12

The Cottage Garden Stylized

The Farmland, and the cottage garden, must be thought of in our context as aspects of the 'nature' of the English countryside from which garden-makers drew their models. Gertrude Jekyll set the example of making use of cottage themes. Inevitably there followed a sophistication of the primitive style, and cottage themes in great gardens have a pleasing touch of Marie Antoinette playing dairy-maid. The origins of some of the admirable effects achieved by Lutyens and Lloyd at Great Dixter, and Sir Harold and Lady Nicolson at Sissinghurst, must be sought in the cottage garden. And in at least a dozen corners of Highdown the same influence is to be seen at work, even if grander ones predominate. Very often the modification introduced by the artist gardener was in nothing much more than the choice of plant material: an effect achieved in the cottage with a common if still lovely rose was repeated in the great garden with a rare new rose from China.[92]

If it be true that in the better cottage gardens of the later nineteenth-century there were preserved both plants and a natural way of growing them together–in salutary contrast with the flamboyant and expensive horticultural luxuries of the rich, the vulgarities of the great gardens and those of the middle class financially able to imitate them–it is equally true that the cottager's unwittingly good example could not help to purify upper-class gardening until an influential gardener took action in the matter. This would have to be someone who could see the merit in the cottage garden; could deduce from it some widely applicable rules; and could then impose his or her ideas at a higher social level than that of the cottager.

That gardener appeared in the person of Miss Gertrude Jekyll, who was born in 1843 and died in 1935. She was a lady–perhaps 'gentlewoman' would be a better word–of wide reading and culture, naturally musical but also musically educated in the graphic arts; literary and educated in

Both the cottage and garden at STYAL, CHESHIRE, have been transmuted to conform to the vision of a rustic paradise fostered by William Robinson and Gertrude Jekyll.

English Cottage Gardens

letters. She was very interested in and practised some of the old cottage crafts. She loved flowers, trees and gardens and was learned in all of them. Moreover, what she knew about them came not merely from books, although she must have read both botany and horticulture, but from familiarity with the cottage gardens, and the larger gardens too, of Surrey, her own county.

It is typical not only of the woman herself, but also of her upbringing, and it is likewise representative of the influence of pre-Raphaelite ideas on the class of well-educated gentlefolk to which she belonged, that when Gertrude Jekyll made up her mind to become a professional artist she did not confine herself to painting or any other 'fine art', but also thought, felt and practised as a craftsman. She travelled

The Cottage Garden Stylized

CHIPPING CAMPDEN,
GLOUCESTERSHIRE
The drystone walling of
the Cotswolds has
always encouraged the
growth of rock plants.
Right A late debased
example of the folly in
the popular form of a
diminutive windmill at
WOODBASTWICK,
NORFOLK.

widely in Europe, became a skilled gilder while she was in Italy, and wherever she went she studied flowers and gardens as well as artefacts.

One of Miss Jekyll's crafts was gardening; and her interest in it was so much stimulated by one of the most remarkable gardeners and garden writers of his time, that it came to dominate the rest. The man in question, the giant of the post-Loudon–Paxton epoch, was William Robinson. It will be necessary to say a little about him, for although his influence on the cottage garden was only indirect, its influence on him was, through Gertrude Jekyll, considerable.

Like so many remarkable gardeners – Capability Brown and Joseph Paxton to take two examples – William Robinson was born (1838) a 'cottager', in Ireland, his parents being Protestants but, socially, very far from members of the Ascendancy, for they were extremely poor. William started his working life as a garden boy in the grand gardens of a clerical baronet, the Rev. Sir Henry Hunt Johnson-Walsh. By the time he was twenty-one he had become head gardener and was in charge of a large range of hothouses full of expensive exotic plants. It seems that he must have had a very bitter row with his employer, for that is the only possible explanation of his extraordinary conduct when, on a night of severe frost, he drew the fires of the hothouse boilers, opened the lights, and fled to Dublin. There he went to see David Moore, the Director of Glasnevin, the National Botanic Garden: what he told Moore is not known, but Moore gave him a letter of recommendation to Robert Marnock, Director of the Royal Botanic Society's gardens in Regent's Park, London. Marnock engaged him, and two years later he was put in charge of the gardens' herbaceous collections. This entailed care of the English native collection, and Robinson took to plant collecting in the countryside. This practice was to have two consequences for the future of English gardening: he conceived a great love for wild flowers and the nature of the English countryside; and an idea for what came to be called 'wild' gardening, a kind of stylized imitation of the natural scene. This, although he may not have realized it, entailed a harking back to the gardening of the early Middle Ages in one of its aspects, that of the 'flowery mead'.

From his observations he gradually conceived a vision of a garden contrived as part of the natural scene but embellished by the choice and delightful representatives of the flora of the other temperate parts of the world – from China to South America.[93]

English Cottage Gardens

Thatch and the equally trim, immensely thick, roof-high hedge, both continuing ancient traditions, conspire together in this Cotswold front garden at CHIPPING CAMPDEN to suggest a mammoth nest, a hyperbolical image of home and rusticity.

It is very much to the point that, in his wanderings about the countryside in his search for specimen plants, Robinson also saw a great many cottage gardens and in them saw miniatures of his conception of a 'natural' garden; and that this must have prepared him for Gertrude Jekyll's ideas, when they met, and for their influence on him. It is equally to our point that he was studying academic botany to such effect that he was elected a Fellow of the Linnaean Society; writing down what he saw and felt about plants and gardens to such effect that he made himself into a first-rate journalist; and teaching himself French to such effect that he was chosen by the great nursery firm of Veitch and by *The Times* to be their Paris representative at the Paris Exhibition of 1867.

Like Gertrude Jekyll, Robinson travelled; but unlike her

The Cottage Garden Stylized

he did it on foot, and in 1870, when he was thirty-two, he published the book which soon established him as a successful man in his chosen field: *Alpine Flowers for English Gardens*. He went to America; he wrote a book called *The Wild Garden*, devoted to his idea of a garden as a planting of 'plants of other countries, as hardy as our hardiest wild flowers, in places where they will flourish without further care or cost'.

Robinson detested formal gardening, although he made exceptions for superlative examples; he detested all that Paxton stood for and what suburban and some cottage gardeners had just got around to doing; he called it 'pastry-work gardening'. And at last he started a magazine, with his own money: *The Garden*; that was in 1871. It was a paper for the upper-class gardener, and although it had a great deal of

Ferns and ivy, at home in the damp crevisses of the limestone plateau of MALHAM, YORKSHIRE, find themselves in an almost identical environment in a miniature rock garden by the outside stair of a cottage in the village.

influence in the world of horticulture, it was not a great financial success. Eight years later he started another magazine, *Gardening* (subsequently *Gardening Illustrated* and now amalgamated with the *Gardeners' Chronicle*), which was for the small, suburban gardener and remained a great success for many years. It was between these two dates that Robinson met Gertrude Jekyll and was as much impressed by her ideas as she by his. Not long after this meeting, Miss Jekyll designed her first garden, for her mother, in Surrey; later, the first woman to do so, she took to designing gardens professionally, and she did not disdain very small gardens.

She began to write for Robinson's paper, *The Garden*, and as a result her influence on the owners and planters of big gardens became considerable. She accepted Robinson's ideas of natural planting; in part, at least, this was because she had one eye on the kind of cottage garden which had always, in its miniature way, been Robinsonian; indeed, as I have said, Robinson himself had been charmed by it, and it may well be that his idea of a garden had been suggested to him as much by the cottage garden as by the untilled countryside in which he sought specimen plants for the Royal Botanical Society's garden in Regent's Park. But, as an artist, Miss Jekyll was bound to impose a measure of order: colours and forms of flowers and plants must never clash, must always be harmonious; her judgement had been formed by the craftsman's respect for the simplicities, for purity of line, proportion in volumes; she was able, as few other garden artists of her time were able, to select rigourosly from the overwhelming mass of plant material which, by the 1870s and 1880s, was at the gardener's disposal; she was never carried away by this excess of riches.

Now what evidence is there that, through Miss Jekyll's work and influence, the gardening of the rich and of their middle-class emulators really was affected by the cottage garden 'style'–really an anti-style until Miss Jekyll, so to speak, deduced aesthetic laws from it? There is visible evidence in plenty, in the shape and planting of some of the great gardens of the late nineteenth and early twentieth centuries. In this connection, Victoria Sackville-West, one of the finest gardeners and garden writers of our time, had this to say about Lawrence Johnston's garden masterpiece, Hidcote Barton Manor:[94]

Would it be misleading to call Hidcote a cottage garden on a most glorified scale? It resembles a cottage garden or rather a series of cottage gardens in so far as the plants grow in a jumble, flowering shrubs mingling with roses, herbaceous plants with bulbous subjects, climbers scrambling over hedges, seedlings coming up wherever they have chosen to plant themselves. Now in a real cottage garden, where limitations and very often the pattern—for example the curve or straightness of a path leading from the entrance gate to the front door—are automatically imposed upon the gardener; the charming effect is both restrained and inevitable. . . . It is very largely accidental. But in a big garden like Hidcote, great skill is required to secure not only the success of the planting, but the proportions which can best give the effect of enclosure. . . . [95]

The important sentence in this passage is the one about great skill: Gertrude Jekyll was the pioneer of that particular skill, accomplishing for those garden artists who came after her the stylization of the cottage garden. For,

It should never be forgotten that the unquestionable charm of the cottage garden was originally as fortuitous as the charm of a woodland glade. And that sophisticated gardeners who were very far from being cottage gardeners used the cottage garden as a motif in exactly the same spirit as they used the woodland glade as a motif: that is to say that in so far as the cottager planted at random and achieved his effects by accident, his garden was a work of nature and not of art. And there is nothing whatever unselfconscious about Hidcote. . . . [96]

To that opinion, which I wrote a decade ago, I would add again the point I have already made touching the reason for it: in choice of plants and the amount of space given to ornamental and useful plants, the cottager was kept in hand by poverty. It is, traditionally, an artist's best friend, for it forces him to respect the simplicities.

There are, besides Hidcote, other great gardens in which 'Cottage Jekyll' is both apparent and an historical fact. For example, she was a frequent visitor to Nymans, the Messels' great 'paradise' garden in Sussex; there the combination of carefully chosen but random planted spring flowers with exotic shrubs is in her manner, a manner now very generally used. And surely Miss Jekyll must have been hovering over Sissinghurst, as a very old woman, when Victoria Sackvill-West and Harold Nicolson were planning and planting the cottage garden section of the great garden which they made there.

This is literally a cottage garden since it is associated with one of the estate cottages called the South Cottage. But it is a cottage garden in the academic horticultural sense, too, for it is planted to a variety of kinds—shrubs, herbaceous plants, bulbs and corms in close association in the manner developed by

Gertrude Jekyll out of traditional cottage gardening. There is, as in all the great Jekyll gardens, a pleasing touch of what I may perhaps call Marie Antoinette-ism about it. For while the method is that of the cottage gardener, the material is more sophisticated; rare as well as common plants have been used together; the criterion has been beauty and nothing else.[97]

There is a difference not yet discussed, and it is an enormous difference, between the spirit of Hidcote, the spirit of Sissinghurst even at its most cottagey, and the spirit of the poor man's cottage garden. It is the social difference: in England the influence of the class structure of society has been paramount on gardening as on every other activity. This is regrettable; but it is a fact which it would be foolish to ignore. The gulf between the real and the stylized cottage garden is wide, and I make no apology for here paraphrasing what I have written elsewhere on this subject, and at the same time enlarging on it: the real cottage garden, the poor man's garden whether in the country or in a suburb, cannot help expressing, unwittingly no doubt, even fortuitously, a spirit of community: historically – remember Larkrise – it was one of a number side by side in a hamlet or village, later a suburban street. In it the cottager, and his wife, did not plant only what they pleased, but what they had to. They gardened in competition with their neighbours, but also in a sort of unconscious collaboration with them. The 'cottage' gardens which together compose Hidcote, and which are some part of other great gardens, are artificially enclosed. Now hedges or fences notwithstanding, enclosed is what a real cottage garden never is; it belongs as much to the road which passes it as to the house. Humphry Repton, writing about the making of his own cottage garden, makes this point: how pleasant and neighbourly it is for the cottage gardener to watch the life of his village, the passing life of the road. And both there and elsewhere in his writings he reproves the exclusiveness, the excesses of privacy marking the separation between class and class, indulged in by so many of the great land-owning gentry and noblemen for whom he had made beautiful gardens. Those great men wanted no sight of their poor neighbours; and most of them would not even let those neighbours cross their parks.

It is curious, in a man of such sensibility, that Repton never refers to the other side of this coin; if it is pleasant and wholly human for the cottager working in his garden to be in touch with the life of his village and the traffic of the road, it is even more pleasant for the neighbours and the traveller to

CHIPPING CAMPDEN, GLOUCESTERSHIRE, is remarkable for memorable examples of cottage topiary. Among them this huge cross is especially striking for its rarity and its symbolism, so much more obviously religious than the commonly occurring cock.

look in upon the serene order of cottage gardens, on the flowers and rows of well-tended vegetables, the apple tree in flower or fruit. In our own time, hundreds of thousands of little gardens are open to the public in a sense that not even the great gardens of people who let them be seen are open.

In one sense, no doubt, time and the internal combustion engine have vindicated the lovers of privacy and put Repton in the wrong. What was pleasant for the cottage or suburban gardener whose garden lay open to the passing traveller in the early and mid nineteenth century is now, in its thunderous noise, fume and ill-temper, very unpleasant indeed; the other side of the coin remains unchanged; one of the chief pleasures of motoring in crowded England is the spectacle, even on hundreds of miles of major roads which must be hell to live on, of prettily planted and well cared for little gardens.

The cottage garden and the small suburban garden is as much the passing traveller's as it is the owners; is as much a part of the village, hamlet or suburb, as it is the owner's private property. It is, in short, a common rather than a private amenity, and as such it harks back to a time when the idea of community was not obscured by the cult of the individual mind and spirit. But today Repton would not be justified in reproving excesses of garden privacy: the strains of living in an overcrowded country have completely changed the conditions; and hell really is other people.

The cottage garden is both unsecret and a thing of use, as much so as the cottage itself, or of its furniture: and a thing of use cannot, by a definition first insisted upon by Alexander Pope, be a work of fine art, for a work of art must exist for its own sake only and be self-justifying. But the Jekyll cottage garden does just that. There is the great difference.

A relatively late example of what Gertrude Jekyll's transformation of an economic accident into a garden style has meant to English gardening can be seen in the greatest of England's modern gardens, Dartington Hall. I have elsewhere described that garden as a harmonious synthesis of all the principal garden styles in the English tradition – Anglo-Italian, Anglo-French, Landscape, Picturesque, Gardenesque. The cottage tradition is to be seen in the flower borders; but again it is the cottage border stylized; strict attention has been paid to colours asociations, habit of plant associations, leaf-form associations. The Dartington borders are a good example of the art which conceals art, not of artlessness.

Miss Jekyll's influence in introducing a style based partly on the old cottage garden and partly on the Robinsonian

The ornamental foliage of this garden at BLAISE, SOMERSET, as exotic as the Picturesque rough bark of the cottage walls, was inspired by the townsman's example.

The Cottage Garden Stylized

wild garden, and partly on her own original conception of a garden, was greater by reason of her writings for *The Garden* and in general her association with Robinson, whose influence on the shape of English gardening was for a time paramount, than by reason of her own work as a garden designer. Nevertheless, her practical work also made its impression. When she came to build herself a house and make a garden, she shared the work of designing both with Edwin Lutyens; each learnt from the other. Thus when Lutyens helped Nathaniel Lloyd to lay out his garden at Great Dixter, one of the half-dozen most accomplished garden works of this century, he did so with what he had learnt from Miss Jekyll in mind: and perhaps Great Dixter could be as validly described as a series of cottage gardens,

The garden at SAFFRON, WALDEN, ESSEX, (*left*) and this at SHOTTERY, WARWICKSHIRE, with its conspicuous golden rod (solidago) are both stylized versions of the cottage garden tradition.

English Cottage Gardens

albeit very grand ones, as could Hidcote. And gardens like Great Dixter influenced the style of laying out and planting medium-sized country gardens and large suburban gardens; they, in their turn, influenced, within the limits set by scale, the planting of small gardens. A curious case of the full circle.

But the small suburban gardens were slower to change, excepting in certain details. Limitations on what could be done were imposed not only by scale, but by the small suburban gardener's conditions of life. Clerk or artisan, he was a hard-working man who could give his garden only a few hours at weekends; and the jobbing gardener whom he might employ for a couple of hours a week had very limited skill and knowledge. Urban air pollution, the terrible smogs of the Victorian and Edwardian periods, also imposed limits

Left and right Once stylized, cottage garden practice could be adapted to public amenity uses such as decorating streets and railway stations as here at SOUTH KENSINGTON, LONDON.

The Cottage Garden Stylized

on the choice of plants. A sort of debased Loudon-Paxton bastard style which was remarkably dull was slowly to give way to the more free-hand gardening of the Surrey school.

The features which were a part of the later Jekyll-style medium-sized garden were taken into the cottage garden and the suburban garden: the herbaceous border; and the rock garden. Perhaps the herbaceous border was originally suggested by the pleasing confusion of plants in the old cottage garden, and then sophisticated by deliberate design and by careful choice of plant material. Although we now regard the herbaceous border as very extravagant in labour, at the time of its adoption into small gardens it was relatively cheap in that respect, for what it replaced was the very time-consuming business of 'bedding-out'. The rural cottage garden was much less affected by such changes, for 'bedding out' does not seem to have been widely accepted by the cottager. It was favoured for decades by the suburban gardener, because 'bedding out' plants were hawked by barrow men about the suburban streets and could easily be bought at one's own back door.

Rock, or alpine, gardening has been taken up by the small gardener only in our own time; it was preceded by what became a familiar and unattractive feature of tens of thousands of suburban gardens, and some cottage gardens: the rockery. Rockeries are described in the *Gardeners' Magazine*, in the year 1831, reprovingly, as '... a hillock of flints and fused bricks', and many such lingered on well into our own times, with a few miserable ferns and perhaps a miraculously surviving hart's tongue fern of the millions which were dug up in the west country by enthusiastic amateur gardeners, and which died on the way back to the east. And yet, the right principles of rock-garden making were already well understood almost a century before Reginald Farrer published his since classic book on the subject:

The grand difficulty in rockwork is to form and maintain a particular character or style in the disposition of the masses: and the only way to conquer this difficulty is to observe the manner in which masses of rock are disposed in nature, or rather in such isolated scenes as are admired by men of taste, and especially painters, and here the study of geology will assist both the painter and the gardener.[98]

Limestone from the surrounding countryside is used at THREPLAND, YORKSHIRE, in the rock garden tradition inaugurated by three Austrian princes.

The pioneers of good rock gardening were three Austrian princes who, late in the eighteenth century, had an alpine rock garden constructed on the Gloriette slope of the great Schönbrunn Park by Heinrich Schott, Curator of the

English Cottage Gardens

Imperial Gardens: the three princes were the Archdukes Johann, Anton and Rainier von Habsburg, and their garden was part of an attempt to form, at Schönbrunn, a complete *Flora Austriaca* collection. Somewhat later, Franz Maly, curator of the gardens at another imperial palace, the Obere Belvedere, started a rock garden there, and when Schott died the Schönbrunn collection was transferred there. This was the beginning of the Alpengarten im Belvedere, today one of the more perfect alpine gardens in the world.

In Maly's rockwork the intention is clear to represent symbolically certain kinds of alpine peaks and sheer rock faces. Maly was far in advance of the rock gardeners of, for example, the Edinburgh Botanic, at about the same time ... and this was so even though Maly was influenced by 'Gothic' baroque, so that by comparison with later, naturalistic style in rock gardening

A miniature Alpine garden in KENSINGTON, LONDON.

The Cottage Garden Stylized

some of his work at Belvedere, still preserved, looks grotesque. Moreover some of it is very clumsy; for example his practice of little 'swallow's nests' of stone and mortar on the rock faces, to hold some of the plants.[99]

In England, the first serious work in rock gardening was done for scientific botanical purposes by William Forsyth at the Chelsea Physic Garden. But the best rock garden in Britain–in the mid nineteenth century and ever since–was in the Edinburgh Botanic Garden; and it was much improved during the curatorship of James McNab. The *Gardeners' Chronicle* described it in 1875 as, ' . . . the largest and most varied rock garden we have ever seen, and the most fascinating'. At that time it contained 4,000 plants.

Although, as we have seen, good theory was not lacking as early as 1831, good practice was long wanting, especially in the

The paving at TEMPLE SOWERBY, CUMBERLAND, though 'crazy', is of local stone, providing the right setting for the plants along its edges.

The Cottage Garden Stylized

Left Rocks, gnome, lighthouse and pool, all the 'art' of the Picturesque landscape garden crowded into one tiny triangle at MELLS, SOMERSET.
Below The same tradition rendered with more gusto and abandon at ASHWELL, HERTFORDSHIRE.

small gardens. William Robinson's *Alpine Flowers for English Gardens* stimulated interest in rock gardens, and slowly practice began to improve, but it was Reginal Farrer who, early in the twentieth century with his book *My Rock Garden*, forwarded this branch of gardening more than any other man. That book was published in 1907 and was followed in 1919 by his monumental *The English Rock Garden*.

From the old cottage garden Gertrude Jekyll borrowed the charm of natural simplicity and from it she produced a garden style. The deliberate practice of 'natural' simplicity in gardening, including rock gardening, at last made the cottage garden self-conscious. Although very many such gardens were still planted at random, the element of design imposed by taste, and not merely by considerations of convenience, became important.

[13]
A Stylized
Cottage Garden

The cottage garden stylized has become one of the possible styles which the sophisticated gardener with a small house or converted cottage in town, suburb or country may use. If he is wise he will not attempt to do what the real old country cottager, originator of the style, did: that is, plant at random. In fact it probably cannot be done; for once a craft has become self-conscious as a consequence of intelligent study, the practitioner is aware of how the best effects were obtained without thought by the old gardeners, and the worst mistakes made; and he is thus obliged, by his own awareness, to do his work deliberately. What this means in practice is that a sophisticated gardener making a cottage garden is, willy-nilly, working in the spirit of an eighteen-century landscape gardener making one of the great picturesque gardens: those artists, Capability Brown, Humphry Repton at their head, made works of gardening art after nature; but they were not to be found in nature, and were as much works of art as a landscape painting.

The cottage style is not, at the present time, much favoured in either town or country, and still less in the suburbs. Small gardens are either in no style at all or they tend to be based on one of a small number of almost standardized miniaturizations of one of the grand classic styles; models of such gardens are to be seen every year at the Royal Horticultural Society's Chelsea Flower Show, and it is remarkable how successful designers have been in scaling down the major features of great gardens. The Italianate, with geometrical layout, paved surfaces, an urn or other artefacts, clipped evergreens, small trees in tubs or vases, few but choice flowers, has, in our time, a great deal to commend it: it is a garden style for living and playing in, not simply for looking at. But more popular with English gardeners, because it gives more scope for plantsmanship and more colour, are miniature landscape-gardenesque or, as

Plant training for decoratives effect is still a fashionable element of the stylized cottage garden. A spectacular example of pyracantha at WELLS, NORFOLK.

A Stylized Cottage Garden

I have called them elsewhere, 'paradise' gardens: central is a lawn with the wavy edges which are *de rigueur*, defining surrounding borders of flowering shrubs with a small number of herbaceous perennials; there will be one or two small flowering trees, perhaps a small group of ornamental conifers, and some rock or peat work for alpine shrubs and perennials and bulbs.

The contemporary style has yet to be seen in English gardens; those in some of the newer lower density housing estates, designed by good garden designers or by architects, are modern in the treatment of garden buildings, paths and play areas, and occasionally of decorative artefacts; but they are not 'abstract' gardens. I know of no miniaturization, for the small garden, of the kind of abstract gardens which that great garden artist Roberto Burle Marx, the Brazillian painter, has made in Rio de Janeiro, in Brasilia and in other South American cities. To the best of my belief, his are the first attempts, in gardening, to practise abstract art since the Japanese Zen dry-landscape gardens of the ninth to eleventh centuries, those gardens composed of raked sand and a few rocks grouped symbolically in a very ancient religious tradition, and disposed with exquisite art. But it is fair to say that great difficulties would confront the would-be abstract artist in English gardening: the forms and habits of temperate zone, cold climate plants are not congruous with the shapes and textures of contemporary wall architecture or sculpture; nor would an abstract garden be congruous with English styles in domestic architecture, least of all with cottage architecture.

To return to the uses of the cottage garden style which has emerged as a result of deliberate study of the cottage garden with no style but much charm: curiously enough, the best representatives of this style which I have seen during the last few years have all been the gardens of urban, terrace cottages, chiefly in London. There are many streets of eighteenth- and early nineteenth-century cottages, built originally for the working classes but converted to modern middle-class use by clever architects, in the boroughs of Kensington, Chelsea and Fulham, for example, in which one can see most admirable examples of stylized cottage gardens. A good case in point is Gordon Place, off Church Street, Kensington.

The real cottage garden had, as we have seen, a great many vegetables; in the stylized version these are, as a rule, but not invariably, eliminated. They are often retained in country cottage gardens; properly tended, rows of cabbages are decorative, and there is no reason why scarlet runner

Window-box and bird table, climbing rose and clematis and a careless profusion of plants of old and new varieties make this little front space at TRUNCH, NORFOLK, a perfect synthesis of the traditional and the stylized cottage garden.

beans should not now, as in the past, be used as ornamental climbers and still provide the cottager with a crop of beans. An asparagus bed is decorative if well tended throughout most of the growing season; and fruit trees which bear fruit are just as ornamental as those 'flowering' cherries, crabs and ornamental pears and peaches which do not. However, the tendency is to eliminate vegetables from the small urban and suburban garden; and from the middle-class country cottager's garden as well.

The designer of a stylized cottage garden in the old manner must begin by putting aside curvilinear layout–derived at many removes from the serpentine designs of Capability Brown–in the shaping of paths, lawn-edges and the edges of borders, and go back to straight-line geometry and hard edges. Suppose the commonest case: a rectangular plot of the order of 400 to 800 square yards. The path from gate to door should be straight, dividing the plot into two parts which may be equal but may not. A path of equal width should cross that at right angles to divide the plot into four. These paths may be of gravel; they may, in a stone district, be of crazy paving, although it is an ugly style and should be avoided where possible; the very best material for a stylized cottage garden is unquestionably brick. Bricks in path-making should never be laid flat, broad side up, but always on edge, even though that means using twice as many of them; they must be laid on a firmly consolidated and levelled base, not necessarily in a concrete bed, though that will eliminate weeds. The bricks can be mortared together or not–you may want to grow stonecrops and other tiny ornamental plants in the cracks. They can be laid in dutch bond, like a wall, but it is prettier to lay them in straight lines, or best of all in a simple pattern, herringbone for example. It may be expedient to lay further paths, for example all round the house itself or along one or two of its sides; in that case either holes, or a narrow bed, should be left for the planting of wall climbers and trained fruit trees. A narrow border is best, because it can be used for herbaceous plants and bulbs as well; such borders against brick or stone walls dry out very easily and need a lot of irrigation, but their advantages outweigh their snags.

The junction of the two paths, one on the gate-door axis, the other at right angles to it, can be a *rond-point*; that is a circle or square of bricks six or eight feet in diameter. This can in due course be covered with a little *gloriette* of iron or woodwork, over which will be trained flowering climbers,

A Stylized Cottage Garden

such as roses, honeysuckles or clematis which are all congruous with the theme; or even a grapevine, not seriously incongruous, for many old cottagers cultivated a vine. Because of the prevalence of the fungus diseases of the genus *Vitis*, it is unwise to plant Old World vines (cultivars of *Vitis vinifera*); it is now possible to obtain grapevines which are hybrids between good Old World cultivars and disease-resistant American species: the hybrid Seyve-Villard 5·276 is, for instance, both resistant to the fungus diseases and bears very handsome bunches of green to amber grapes.

The *rond-point* at the junction of the two main paths can be decorative: it can be of pebble-work instead of brick; or bricks can be laid in a wheel pattern to form spokes and rim, and segments filled with pebble-work. That kind of thing is in keeping with the cottage theme. Naked concrete should never be used; it is always ugly. Lawn-grass paths and *rond-points* are pretty but impractical.

The cottage wall backing the garden should be equipped with properly cemented vine-eyes to carry taut wires for the training of wall plants, or to hold steel, plastic or wooden trellis in place. This advance preparation of the wall will eliminate a great deal of trouble later. Walls facing south, south-east or south-west can be used for trained fruit trees which are both ornamental and useful: the purist will stick to pears; they are handsomer trees, they are easier to prune, and they are less troubled with pests and diseases than, say, peaches. Flowering climbers should be honeysuckles, the older kinds of clematis, jasmines or old roses. Wistaria is a wall-plant rarely seen in the classic cottage garden, but perhaps only a strict purist would exclude it on that account. On the other hand, Virginia creeper is quite out of place; by association, it is a suburban plant, but apart from that consideration it is too vigorous for a cottage wall.

After laying down the paths and attending to the preparation of the walls, the designer of a cottage garden should give his attention to another permanent feature: hedges and edges. First, the three sides of the garden not backed by the cottage wall should be surrounded by a hedge, of the kind which can be clipped hard. No doubt the least troublesome hedge is privet, but it is rarely beautiful, and the best hedges are cheerful evergreens. If a deciduous plant is to be used, then let it be the sweet-scented eglantine. The densest and handsomest hedges are holly or yew and they should be preferred if the gardener is either very patient and not too old; or rich enough to buy relatively large pot-grown plants.

If holly is used, a very pleasing 'tapestry' effect can be obtained by planting a certain number of gold, silver and tricolour variegated hollies among the green ones, but the green should predominate. Yew is not as slow-growing as is commonly supposed, at least in its youth.

The gardener who is neither rich nor patient can make his peripheral hedges with a fast-growing cypress. True, it is not an 'old-fashioned' plant, but this is another case where expediency can be allowed to override purism. *Cupressus macrocarpa* should never be used; it always and quite soon starts to become bare at the lower end of the trunks. The plant to use is *Chamaecupressus leylandii*, a bigeneric hybrid known as Leyland cypress: it is a cheerful bright green; its foliage has a most pleasing texture surpassed only by that of the Italian cypress which is not reliably hardy in the average climate of Britain; it is very fast-growing indeed; and it is always clad to the ground.

The paths can either be hedged or planted with edging dwarf shrubs. Low hedges are handsome and make a garden more interesting by dividing it into compartments. Moreover, they can be trained high to form arches at the points where the hedge has to be pierced for access to the borders or paths. Beech is a possible hedging plant for this purpose; true, it is deciduous, but clipped beech retains the dead leaves until spring, and as they are a bright reddish brown

The Picturesque style finds its last decadent expression in the suburban garden. A memorable example at MITCHAM, SURREY.

A Stylized Cottage Garden

and of an attractive texture, they are decorative. In the warmest parts of the country the tiny-leaved *Lonicera nitida* makes an excellent, close-textured, low hedge. It is not quite hardy. If beech is used, a beautiful tapestry effect can, again, be obtained by planting some of the copper beeches with the green ones.

But low edging plants will commonly be preferred to hedges for the interior of the garden, and are perhaps more in keeping with the old cottage theme. The plant which comes first to mind is, of course, dwarf box; but there are other interesting possibilities. Paths can be edged with lavender which can be kept clipped to a neat rounded cushion whose silvery-grey colour is in pleasing contrast with the red of the brick paths: the best cultivar for the purpose is 'Hidcote', easier to keep in shape, naturally dwarfed, while its flowers, almost as sweet-scented as the type, are of a much richer colour. Lavender edging can be maintained short and bushy and full and prevented from growing leggy, by clipping it over quite closely after the flowers have been gathered or have withered on the plants. Path edging can be made with a number of other herbs, santolina for one, or the curry-plant or even chives. Best of all is rue, but in that case only the cultivar called 'Jackman's Blue' should be used, for its colour is most striking. Careful pruning twice a year is necessary to keep a rue edge in shape.

A very beautiful path edge, or rather something between a hedge and an edge, can be made with rosemary: close-set, the plants starve each other, and so help to prevent excessive growth. Rosemary can be clipped round or square, and anything between eighteen and forty inches high. But it is not absolutely hardy in all parts of Britain, and exposed to east winds during hard frost, may be killed or at least injured, thus producing unsightly gaps in the hedge for a couple of years. There is a very pretty golden-variegated rosemary whose leaves are splashed and straked with golden yellow; it is easier to find in Ireland than in England; but it is an old cottage garden plant and would be very much in place.

One of the four divisions of the garden should be given over to an apple or pear tree. It will be a principal feature and should therefore be chosen, sited and planted with care, so placed that its shadow will do least harm to other plants in the garden. The apple and pear trees sold by nurseries for small gardens are grafted onto very dwarfing stocks in order to keep them small even at maturity, and to make them crop early in their lives. This is not the kind of tree required for

Grotesque descendants of the deities and nymphs of such great gardens as Stourhead and Rousham at WELLS, NORFOLK.

English Cottage Gardens

Vestiges of the Roman garden in a London basement area.

a stylized, old-fashioned cottage garden. There are a number of things to be sure of before buying the tree: first, that it is grafted onto a rootstock which will make it a big tree; secondly, that since one might as well have only prime fruit from one's own garden, that it is a good kind – one of the aromatic apples of the Cox's orange pippin class if it is an apple; and if a pear, then a really fine one like Doyenne du Comice. But most good apples and pears are wholly or partly self-sterile; that is to say, they need a pollinator if they are to set fruit well. If only one tree can be planted in the garden and there are none of the same kind but another variety in a neighbouring garden, then the nurseryman should be persuaded to graft one branch of the young tree over to a suitable pollinator.

A possible and correct treatment of the garden division given over to the fruit tree is to grass down all but a narrow border for perennials, and after planting spring-flowering bulbs to grow through the grass. The bulbs should be chosen with regard for scale: thus, the native daffodil, *Narcissus pseudonarcissus*, will be right; the big show daffodils all wrong; but, the anachronism notwithstanding, some of the new semi-miniatures could certainly be used. Snow-drops, of course; but it is important to get stock for planting while the plants are still in green leaf or even in flower; so planted, snowdrops will take almost anywhere, whereas dormant bulbs rarely give satisfactory results. The native bluebell is too big for this small lawn, but scillas can be used instead. For tulips and crocus, stick to the botanical species which again are nearer the right size. Cyclamen can be grown in grass, notably *Cyclamen vernum*, *C. coum* and, above all, *C. neapolitanum*, which flowers in autumn. All bulb flowers should be in small groups or drifts of one kind; spotty planting is an abomination. But let each group be random planted; it is impossible to plant deliberately at random. So the planter stands with a double handful of bulbs, throws them down, and plants each where it falls, firmly resisting the temptation to rearrange the bulbs.

Then there is the narrow border round this flowering lawn. Plants chosen for it should be of the old-fashioned kinds, of course: Crown Imperials and Madonna lilies might be planted where the border is sunny. And this part of the garden might well be used for the other three 'cottage' lilies, that is the lilies which are congruous not only by their association, but in their looks. As well as *Lilium candidum* (the madonna lily), there is, first of all, *L. martagon*. The only way to get virus-free plants of the first is by growing them from seed. It is a slow business, but not so slow as raising martagons from seed, for that takes seven years to the flowering stage. Martagon bulbs are free from virus disease, or resistant; but dear. Then there is *L. chalcedonicum*, the scarlet martagon; and finally, the orange *L. bulbiferum* var. *croceum*, whose colour is difficult to associate with any other.

If incongruities are to be avoided, the same care must be exercised in the choice of all the plants for the whole garden. Hybrid tea and floribunda roses must be excluded, of course; they would be very out of place. This is not simply a matter of dates: the flowers are the wrong shape, the foliage is wrong, the habit of the bushes is very wrong indeed. But this does not mean that all modern roses should be excluded; some of the hybrid musk roses would be congruous, although quite new. And some of the climbers which might not be thought of as cottage roses look very well in the setting suggested, for example, Zepherine Drouin, or the Paul's climbers, Scarlet and Lemon Pillar. But the gardener who wanted to stick strictly to his theme would plant such roses as *Rosa alba* cultivars – Maiden's Blush, the reddish-purple Rose de Rescht, and others of that race.

As I have said, the earliest man-made roses to become 'old-fashioned' after having been fashionable in the gardens of the great, were the *centifolia*, *damascena* and *gallica* cultivars, followed by the Bourbons. With that in mind, the cottage garden stylist will plant such roses as Gros chou d'Hollande, Fantin Latour, Madame Hardy, the lavender Château Gaillard, Blush Damask, York and Lancaster or *Rosa mundi*, Camaieux and Belle de Crecy. There are too many to list; not all are really very old, but they have the right habit, the right look. Moss roses are suitable, of course, but not the *rubiginosas*. As for 'ramblers', most of them seem out of place, but perhaps they may be admitted.

Probably a whole division of these cottage garden roses will be planted together. Between them and the lavender hedge there will be room for a band of perennials. Some of the old flag irises would be congruous, the older short-spurred aquilegias, canterbury bells and some other campanulas, the big white daisies, *Chrysanthemum maximum*; but certainly not, for example, Michaelmas daisies.

What about those relative newcomers, the big autumn-flowering chrysanthemums, dahlias and gladioli. The only admissible gladiolus would be the species *byzantinus*, an old cottage garden plant. The gardener who is not too strict will pro-

English
Cottage Gardens

bably admit some of the lovely little species from South Africa, though they would be an anachronism; but the big 'improved' or 'florists' gladioli must, of course, be excluded, unless they be grown in a row, for cutting, in the kitchen garden.

There is a good reason, if you are a stickler for history, to admit the big chrysanthemums, the incurved Chinese cultivars, to cottage gardens. I have above discussed the cottagers' work, in the north country, on auriculas, ranunculas, pinks and some other garden flowers; later, in some of the coal-mining districts, the miners took up the chrysanthemum, and held annual shows, and produced magnificent specimen flowers, using in their cultivation a gentle skill and delicacy of taste which, immanent in all men, are frustrated in most. But this was a very highly specialized skill, practised in the tiny terrace cottage gardens of a small number of small neighbourhoods, and the fact is that these chrysanthemums look wrong in stylized cottage gardens. As for the dahlias, again, no: they could be grown, like the gladioli, in the kitchen garden, in rows for cutting.

Of the common herbacious perennial favourites, some present difficulties. Although Russel was a cottager, his lupins will not do, nor in my view any lupins. The monstrous modern delphiniums are awful in any case, and would be excluded on ordinary grounds of taste; but the little old ones might be grown. Pinks, carnations, bleeding-heart, hellebores–yes, of course. But not, for example, red-hot pokers, for our garden is not simply a matter of history, of dates, but of associations, ideas. And since it is a question of stating a clear theme to arouse certain sentiments, a certain kind of nostalgia, and of trying to reconstruct a piece of the past, the same rule will be kept for flowering shrubs; in their case it will be found much more restrictive. We can admit lilacs, and having done so might as well include cultivars which, strictly speaking, do not belong in a cottage garden. We can also admit the mock orange, *Philadelphus*, which reached us from south Europe early in the sixteenth century and has been in cottage gardens certainly since the early eighteenth century. Again, one might as well have the best representatives, rather than the inferior old ones, for the differences are in detail not in habit and are not enough to shock. By the same rule we must completely exclude the whole genus *Rhododendron*, for although some had reached England in the seventeenth century, they were never, excepting in Cornwall, cottage garden plants; *Camellia*, too, is out. Herbaceous paeonies are very much in place in a cottage garden of the

The ultimate vulgarization of the garden inscription.

A Stylized Cottage Garden

kind we are making, especially the old, blowsy red, and white doubles. But we cannot admit moutans, the tree paeonies. The climbers we have already discussed.

This kind of cottage garden can perfectly well admit a decorated garden seat; but no purely 'artistic' ornament is in place. The history of figurative art in gardens is a very ancient one indeed, and it is excessively complicated. To recapitulate it briefly and simply: it began in the proto-civilizations of the Near East with religious shrines and it also developed in very ancient Greece when the sacred grove, with either a sacred spring or the figure of a divinity, turned into a garden. In this, as in other ways, the Romans copied the Greeks and set up the figures of gods or demi-gods in their garden groves; in due course, these became more or less secularized, and were regarded as sentimental decorations rather than objects of reverence. In the completely alien Eastern civilizations something similar in spirit but different in terms occurred. The great water-eroded stones which the ancient Chinese set up in their great landscape gardens were early looked upon as housing benevolent forces or spirits. But in time they were treated as objects of *vertu;* the best of them all came from the bottom of a particular lake, cost an immense amount of money, were admired and criticized as works of art, and at last changed hands at such fantastic prices that ingenious craftsmen found it worth while to make fakes.

In Japan, crane-and-tortoise artefacts of various kinds were absolutely essential in all gardens; they were worshipful symbols of longevity. Most improbably, I found a magnificent old specimen, although probably not earlier than the fourteenth century, in the 'English' garden of a ranchero in the middle of Argentina. These crane-and-tortoise groups were at first realistic, later abstract works. The groups of *horai*[100] rocks in the lakes of Japanese gardens, and later in the dry-landscape Zen gardens, represent an ancient Chinese [*sic*] legend also connected with longevity. Other objects of art in Japanese gardens all have religious significance, mostly Zen Buddhist, but some much older (older that is, in Japan). Even the stone lanterns we associate with Japanese gardens are religious symbols, Christian in that case, and very late-comers to Japanese gardens.

Other cultures used quite other kinds of both figurative and abstract art in gardens. In both Mexico and Peru, before the Conquest, plants and animals of goldsmith's and silver-smith's work were mingled with the living specimens in

Another part of the selfconscious, tricked-out cottage garden shown on p. 211. Here it is given another dimension by the cat and the splendid curvilinear east window of LUDHAM parish church, NORFOLK.

gardens and menageries. In the Islamic gardens, pavilions and abstract artefacts were used in place of figures, since the Moslem people took literally the commandment to make unto themselves no graven image.

It would probably be difficult to find an example more remarkable of the slavish way in which Renaissance Europeans copied antiquity than that of their use of the Olympian gods and demi-gods, nymphs and mythical animals, in their gardens. It seems never to have occurred to the Italians and the French, much less to the English and Germans, to replace the Hellenistic with the Christian demi-gods–that is he saints– in their garden groves and niches. There are a few cases, but very few; I have come across only two myself. Perhaps, in the garden at least, they gave expression to a secret yearning for a religion more amusing and less restrictive than Christianity with its harsh, puritanical Semitic undertones.

So, then, the great gardens of every style and culture had works of figurative or abstract art in them; but they were not to be found in small gardens; they could not have been afforded, of course. The cottage garden of the kind we are here stylizing had no such ornaments. In our own century there has been a curious manifestation of one aspect of a culture in decadence–whimsicallty–in the form of gnomes in gardens. The toadstools cast in concrete, the metal and plastic

Cottage garden styles could be adapted to such purposes as pub and tea-room gardens for summer visitors as here at GREAT BRICKHILL, BEDFORDSHIRE.

A Stylized Cottage Garden

storks and rabbits are, in spirit, no worse, of course, than the iron or bronze deer and other creatures in the great gardens of the past; but gnomes, gnomes with comic little faces, fishing in tiny little garden pools with no water in them, are new.

The stylized cottage garden should include a small herb garden, either in the narrow border near the house and in that case on either side of one of the doors; or in some mildly fanciful arrangement such as a cartwheel laid flat, each segment between spokes and rim being planted with a different herb. The classic cottage garden herbs are rosemary, thyme, sage, winter-savory, garlic, parsley, marjoram, fennel, chives coriander, dill, hyssop and mint. The artemisia called either 'southernwood', 'old man', or 'lad's love' is a very pleasant bush to have here and there in the garden, to pinch as you pass; but it is not a classic herb.

There are some other typical features to be included: there should be a big patch of lily-of-the-valley in partial shade, near the house; a group of oenothera and, if you can get the seed, Marvel-of-Peru near to the sitting-room window, for evening fragrance; wall-flowers in spring; a good collection of violets and primroses, of which more will be said, laced pinks and laced polyanthus, both of which can be raised from seed in the first instance; many more of the old perennials, such as phlox and stocks, which I have not yet mentioned; violas, pansies and auriculas.

The collection of old primroses, some of which go back to Elizabethan times, should include some hose-in-hose kinds – the bright yellow Canary Bird, if you can get it, the apricot Lady Lettice and the mauve Lady Molly. But the fully double primroses are prettier, the easiest to get and to grow being the race called Bon Accord: these are fully double flowers like miniature carnations in shape, varying in colour very widely from a true royal-blue, through purple, to a range of reds and mauves; there are also whites, creams and yellows, of course, and even a green-flowered kind, but it is of no great merit. No real old cottage garden would have had all these, or rather as many primroses like these, for the ancient doubles were not of this fine race. But the gardener making an old-fashioned cottage garden can certainly use them all and should, on the other hand, avoid the huge modern polyanthus, though he should have some oxslips. I do not suggest that the primroses be all planted in one place, nor the violet collection, which should include as many kinds of *Viola odorata* as the gardener can find, including the lovely rose-pink Mrs J.J.Astor and the pale yellow *V*.

sulphurea. I never found Parma violets satisfactory in open borders, and in any case they are not cottage flowers.

Of the old 'florists' flowers, *Ranunculus asiaticus* can be grown from seed; the double, pink daisies (*Bellis*) are still sold by some nurseries; stonecrops for paths and walls can be raised from seed. The only *Sempervivum* admissible is the old house leek; but that should certainly be there. Both periwinkles, *Vinca major* and *V. minor* are in place, and very useful for shady corners, although both flower better if partly exposed to the sunshine. *V. minor* is, in many ways, a better plant than the larger-flowered *major*; it is not susceptible to the disease which attacks the latter, and which sometimes wipes out every plant in the garden: it is more truly prostrate; and it has some admirable varieties, one with variegated leaves, one with double, light blue flowers, one with wine-red flowers, some single and some double on the same plant, and some very pretty whites. All belong properly in the cottage garden.

Some of the old cottage flowers, so-called, are far from easy to grow. I have mentioned the madonna lily. I do not think that a cottage gardener in the east of the country should bother with the St Brigid and de Caen anemones unless he can find some really old stock of corms; they have been bred for size and colour and have lost hardiness; they are fairly easy in the west country. The blues, like *Anemone appenina* and *A. blanda* are easy; hardly in place, but they may pass. Japanese anemones are in many cottage gardens but should be avoided; they are out of scale, usually tatty, and never very beautiful.

I have mentioned the restricted range of shrubs which are in character; to them can be added laurustinus; and, among small shrubs, tutsan, the native St John's wort, but not the big hypericums. There is, of course, *Daphne mezereum*, well established in cottage gardens for at least 300 years, for it is a native English plant and early attracted attention by its late winter flowering and its extraordinary colour. It is now by no means easy to keep alive for long; having grown eighteen species of *Daphne*, I found this one far from being the easiest, doubtless for the reason that the plants were easily diseased. However, this daphne is so well worth having in a cottage garden that it is also worth taking a lot of trouble over: plants raised from seed are free from virus disease until they get it from some other, diseased, plant of the same species. Berries are usually plentiful on garden daphnes and the seed germinates readily; so it is not difficult to keep in

hand a reserve of healthy young mezereons–the old vernacular name. The white-flowered variety is well worth
having also. Some gardeners say that the white is more
robust and less liable to die suddenly than the type; I do not
see how it can be, but there it is.

Another daphne which is congruous with the rest of the
cottage garden flora is *D. laureola*, another native; it has not
much beauty, but it is an evergreen and has the great merit
of being able to grow well in the deep shade of trees.

To sum up: the rules for laying out and planting a
pastiche of an old-fashioned cottage garden are straight-
forward. The design should be rectangular and very simple.
The native plant species can be included in the planting, and
every cultivar not later than, say, the middle of the nineteenth century, excepting those which, for whatever reason,
have never been cottage garden plants, have never been
associated with the 'idea' of a cottage garden.

What possible justification can there be for thus deliberately making restrictive rules for the making of a garden?
Only, of course, the one which justifies the acceptance of
rules in any art: by working to a particular theme the
gardener settles, in advance, a considerable part of the
problem of selection of material; and challenges himself to
create a perfect work within the defined limits of a particular
form; the stylized cottage garden style is as good a one as
any to work in, and for the small garden, better than most.

Notes and Sources

1] Amherst, Alicia, in *A History of Gardening in England*, Quaritch, London 1895, quoting Earle's *English Plant Names*.

2] Hyams, E, *Capability Brown and Humphry Repton* Dent, London : Scribner, New York 1970.

3] Original MS : British Museum Cotton Vitellius CIII. There are three other MSS, all dating from the 11th century.

4] Sloane MS, 1686: *The tretyse off housebandry that Mayster Groshe made that whiche was Bishope of Lyc-ll he translate this booke out off frensche in to English.*

5] ibid.

6] ibid.

7] Sloane MS, no.5, sect.3.

8] Halliwell, G.O. (ed.), *Early English Miscellanies* Warton Club, London 1855.

9] See *Archeologia* vol.LIV.

10] It is, of course, untrue that cabbages and such salads as lettuce were not grown in England before the 17th century. 'Introduction' of such vegetables from Holland or elsewhere were only introductions of new and improved varieties.

11] Chaucer, 'The Miller's Tale':
She was wel more blisful to see
Than is the newe perjenete tree.

12] T.D. Lysenko: Soviet biologist, now considered a charlatan but backed by Joseph Stalin, who reconciled biology with Marxism by arguing that a plant could be fundamentally (genotypically) altered by environment.

13] Amherst, op.cit.

14] From *The Form of Cury*.

15] *Five Hundred Pointes of Good Husbandrie*.

16] Amherst, op.cit.

17] ibid, quoting what she describes as "a curious and rare pamphlet" published in London by one Roger Jackson in 1609.

18] Amherst, op. cit.

19] Harrison, W, *Description of Bretaine and England* (ed. Furnival), New Shakespeare Society, part I, book 2, p324.

20] Drummond, J.C, and Wilbraham, A, *The Englishman's Food* Jonathan Cape, London 1939.

21] Parkinson, John. *Paradisi in Sole Paradisus Terrestris, or a garden of all sortes of pleasant flowers*, London (in folio) 1629.

22] Gerard, John, *The Herbal, or General Histoire of Plants* J. Norton, London (in folio) 1597.

23] Vavilov, N.I. *The Origin, Variation, Immunity and Breeding of Cultivated Plants* (trans. K. Starr Chester) Ronald Press, New York 1951.

24] Hill, Thomas, *Gardener's Labyrinth*, London 1608.

25] Lawson, William, *A New Orchard and Garden. Or the Best Way of Planting. With the Country Housewife's Garden*, printed by C. Alsop for R. Jackson, London 1617–18.

26] Googe, Barnaby, *Four Bookes of Husbandrie* London 1578. This was actually a pirated translation of Conrad Heresbach, and as such is not reliable as to what was happening in English practice.

27] Holinshead, Ralph, *Chronicles of England, Scotland and Ireland*, London 1586/7. This edition includes William Harrison's *Description* etc. quoted above.

28] Amherst, op.cit.

29] Vavilov, op.cit.

30] Salaman, R.N. *The History and Social Influence of the Potato*, Cambridge University Press 1949.

31] Monardes, Nicholas (1571). The translation (1577) is entitled *Joyful Newes out of the New World*.

32] In his *Phytopinax* 1596.

33] Serres, Olivier de, *Theatre d'Agriculture et Mesnage des Champs* 1600.

34] Hamilton,E, *American Treasure and the Price Revolution in Spain 1501 to 1650*, Harvard Economic Studies, vol.XLIII, p196. See also his private communication to Salaman in the latter, op.cit.

35] Henze,G. *Notice sur l'introduction et la propagation de la pomme de terre en France et en Europe*, Paris 1886.

36] Salaman, op.cit, p147 *et seq.*

37] See ibid. for a full and detailed study of the reason why Irish social conditions favoured the potato.

38] ibid, p215.

39] Petty, Sir W, *Political Anatomy of Ireland* 1691, p59; and Dunton,J. *Some Account of my Conversation in Ireland in a Letter to an Honoured Lady*, Appendix B, Letter 4, in Mac Lysaght's *Irish Life in the Seventeenth Century* 1939.

40] Clearly connected with the phallic shape of the tuber of *Ipomaea batata*. '*How the devil luxury, with his fat rump and potato finger, tickles these together! Fry, lechery, fry!*' (Shakespeare), *Troilus and Cressida*.

41] Salaman, op.cit., whose source here is Eden, Sir F, *The Statue of the Poor* 1797.

42] Evelyn,John, *Diary* (ed.Wheatley), vol.IV, 1879, p441.

43] Forster,John, *England's Happiness Increased*. The book is dedicated to Charles II.

44] Salaman, op.cit., p451.

45] Young, Arthur, *Annals of Agriculture* vol.XLII, p284.

46] Salaman, op.cit., p465. His source is Eden. op.cit. ref.40 above.

47] White, Gilbert. *The Natural History of Selbourne*.

48] Young, Arthur, *A Six Weeks Tour through the Southern Counties of England and Wales* 1768.

49] Young, Arthur, *A Six Months Tour through the North of England* 1771.

50] Rea, John, *Flora, Ceres and Pomona*, London 1676.

51] See, e.g., Genders, Roy, in *The Cottage Garden*, Pelham Books, London 1969.

52] ibid.

53] Austen, Ralph, *A Treatise of Fruit Trees*, Oxford 1653; and *The Spiritual Use of an Orchard or Garden of Fruit Trees* 1655.

54] Evelyn, John, *Kalendarium Hortense or Gardener's Almanac* 1705.

55] Vavilov, op. cit.

56] Hyams, E., *The Speakin Garden*, Longmans, Green, London 1957.

57] A fact established by Humboldt.

58] Hernández, *Historias*.

59] Thompson, Flora, *Larkrise to Candleford*, Oxford University Press 1945.

60] Amherst, op. cit.

61] See Hyams, E. *The English Garden*, Thames & Hudson, London 1962, and Hyams, E. *Capability Brown and Humphry Repton*, Dent, London, 1970.

62] Repton, Humphry, *Fragments on the Theory and Practice of Landscape Gardening*.

63] Thompson, op.cit.

64] Loudon, J.C, *The Villa Gardener* Second edition (ed. Mrs Loudon), London 1850.

65] Loudon published an edition of Repton's works, with an introduction and biographical notes.

66] By the Royal Horticultural Society.

67] Quoted by Miles Hadfield in *Gardening in Britain*, Hutchinson, London 1960.

68] Hyams, E, *Strawberry Growing Complete*, Faber and Faber, London 1958 and 1962.

69] As a result of this experimental work, autumn strawberries have now become a commonplace on the British markets.

70] According to a National Readership Survey (1969), seven people read every copy of *Amateur Gardening*: of the total readership of about 1·5 million, 374,000 are in the cI income bracket, i.e. are 'cottagers' in country or suburbs; 55 per cent of readers are male, 45 per cent female; the majority are over forty-five years of age.

71] In the Royal Horticultural Society Lindley Library.

72] Anon, quoted by Hadfield in op.cit.

73] Hadfield, op.cit.

74] Loudon, J.C, *Encyclopaedia of Gardening*, London 1822.

75] *Dictionary of Gardening*, Royal Horticultural Society.

76] Named after the Charleston nurseryman, Philipe Noisette, who introduced these roses to Europe through his brother Louis-Claude Noisette, a Paris gardener. Their father had been gardener to Louis XVIII.

77] Hyams, *The English Garden.*

78] Hadfield, op.cit.

79] ibid.

80] Earlier dates have been given, but the history of Japanese gardening seems to me to make them very improbable.

81] *Dictionary of Gardening*, Royal Horticultural Society

82] ibid.

83] Genders, in op.cit., has some interesting brief histories of familiar garden flowers.

84] *Gardeners' Magazine* VI.

85] Hadfield, op.cit.

86] Hyams, E, and MacQuitty, W, *Great Botanical Gardens of the World*, Nelson, London 1969.

87] ibid.

88] Hadfield, op.cit.

89] For a general study of the allotment movement in Britain, see Fay, C.R. and H.C, *The Allotment Movement in England and Wales*, National Allotments Society, London 1942.

90] See Section 22 (1) of the 1922 Allotment Act.

91] Hyams, *The English Garden.*

92] Hadfield, op.cit.

93] Now maintained by the National Trust.

94] From Hyams, *The English Garden.*

95] ibid.

96] ibid.

97] *Gardeners' Magazine* VI.

98] Hyams, E, and MacQuitty, W, *Great Botanical Gardens of the World.*

99] In Japanese Gardening: a group of rocks of specific relative sizes and position to each other recalling a legend of a group of islands inhabited by cranes, tortoises and divine beings enjoying great longevity.

Index

Hooker, Sir William Jackson (1785–1865), botanist, 157
Horehound, 102
Horticultural Journal, 106, 112
Horticultural Societies, 112; influence on small garden, 82, 122; origin of village clubs, 112, 116; class variations between north and south, 116; *see under* Royal
Horticulture, monastic gardeners, 7–8; application of science and technology, 139ff.; *see also* Gardening
Hot-houses, 39; for exotics, 79, 149
Housing, of rural poor, 60, 82; relationship between density and garden activity, 162–3, 166; use of better-than-average farm land, 169; percentage viable for food production, 169
Hoxton, nursery gardens, 79
Hull, 157
Huxley, Anthony, ed. *Amateur Gardener*, 113
Hyacinth, 40, 71; 'florists' flowers', 117, 118
Hyams, Edward, his 'paradise' gardens, 203; *Strawberry Growing Complete*, 108; *Soil and Civilization*, 164
Hybridization, in eighteenth century, 79
Hyocyanus niger, 48
Hypericums, 11, 93, 216
Hyssop, 14, 215

I

Incas, farm and garden crops, 36–7, 48 72; use of guano, 142
India, roses from, 128
Iran, roses from, 128
Ireland, introductions of potatoes, 49, 51–2, 55, 108; agricultural system, 51; anacronistic social system, 52; at war with England, 52; cottage gardens, 61; outbreak of potato blight, 144
Iris, 22, 71, 209
Irish National Botanic Garden, 156–7
Islam, artefacts in gardens, 214
Isope, 37
Italy, Black Death, 3–4; suburban

gardens, 6; introduction of cherries, 20; influence of landscape painting on gardening, 23; influence of *ricami*, 26; use of topiary, 26, 38; and the potato, 49; and the tomato, 72, 75; habitat of sweet peas, 155; influence on small gardens, 194
Ixias, 149

J

Japan, *Rosa multiflora*, 134; plants from, 151, 152, 155; and the chrysanthemum, 152–3; Zen dry-landscape gardens, 203, 213; crane-and-tortoise artefacts, 213
Jasmines, 36, 205
Jeffrey, John, plant collector, 151–2
Jekyll, Gertrude (1843–1935), 1; cottage garden influence, 24, 124, 178, 184, 185, 186, 199; accomplishments, 178–81; influenced by Robinson, 181, 182, 184, 191; gardening art, 184; and gardens of the rich, 184; at Gt Dixter, 191–2
Johnson, George William (1802–86), ed. *Cottage Gardener*, 105–6, 109; and manures, 106; and cottage gardener, 106, 108; and cultivars, 108; class of readers, 112
Johnson, Thomas (*d*.1644), plant collector, 46–7
Johnson-Walsh, Revd Sir Henry Hunt, 181
Johnston, Lawrence, and Hidcote Barton, 184, 186
Judas trees, 93

K

Kale, 3, 101
Keens, Michael, and strawberries, 108
Kent, codling apples, 43; cherries, 44
Kent, William (1684–1748), 1; and landscape gardening, 80
Kew Gardens, Banks and, 121, 149; Directors, 122, 151, 156
Kingdon-Ward, Frank (1885–1958), plant collector, 152
Kitchen gardens, 106; most important crops, 18, 32; development of new varieties, 18, 68; possible source of income, 31–2; changes in

seventeenth and eighteenth centuries, 68, 80; suburban, 93–6
Knight, Thomas Andrew (1759–1838), 109
Kniphophia, 153, 210
Knot, the, 26; pebble and shell edgings, 39
Korea, 152; *Rosa multiflora*, 134
Kymer, Gilbert (*d*.1463), dean of Salisbury, *Dietary*, 15

L

Laburnum, 40, 96
Lambeth, Tradescants' garden, 47, 53
Lancashire, 24; acceptance of potato, 57, 61; Gooseberry clubs, 101, 116; and auriculas, 121
Landscape gardening, artists of, 80; destruction of old plants, 80; influence on small garden, 200, 203
Langland, William (*c*.1332–*c*.1400), 'cherry-time', 20; *Piers Plowman*, 16–7
Lathyrus odorata, 155
Laurel, 3
Laurustinus, 92, 216
Lavender, 11, 37, 84, 102; cultivar Hidcote, 207
Lawes, Sir John Bennet (1814–1900), and agricultural science, 142–4; model co-operative society, 161
Lawson, William (*fl*.1618), and topiary, 37–8
Le Gentil, trns of *The Solitary Gardener*, 79
Le Nôtre, André (1613–1700), garden artist, 23, 24, 78
Leeks, 2, 3, 8, 15, 16, 17, 80; farm and garden yield per acre, 164
Lelamour, John, trns of Macer, 15
Lemons, 70
Lete, Nicholas, plant collector, 46
Lettsom, J. S., Quaker doctor, 104
Lettuce, 3, 15, 16, 80, 101; farm and garden yield per acre, 164
Leyden University, Clusius garden, 21; Botanic Garden, 55
Liebig, Freiherr Justus von (1803–73), soil analysis and plant needs, 142; 'fixes' atmospheric nitrogen, 144
Liger, Louis, trns *of The Retired Gardener*, 79